Legal Issues for the Medical Practitioner

W0016691

David SY Wong

Dedicated to
my beloved wife, Dr Lina Li,
and our three children,
John, Mark and May

Legal Issues for the Medical Practitioner

David Sau-yan Wong

MBBS (HK), FRCS Ed, FRACS, FCSHK, FHKAM,
LLB (Lond), LLM (Lond), PCLL (HK)

香港大學出版社
HONG KONG UNIVERSITY PRESS

Hong Kong University Press
14/F Hing Wai Centre
7 Tin Wan Praya Road
Aberdeen
Hong Kong
www.hkupress.org

ISBN 978-988-8028-98-6

British Library Cataloguing-in-Publication Data
A catalogue record for this book is available from the British Library.

Cover image by David Sau-yan Wong

Printed and bound by Goodrich Int'l Printing Co. Ltd., Hong Kong, China

Contents

About the author

Dr. David Sau-yan Wong (黃守仁醫生) studied at the Diocesan Boys' School in Hong Kong. He then pursued medicine and graduated from the University of Hong Kong in 1982, with the CP Fong Gold Medal and the Gordon King Prize. He was then trained to be a surgeon and has remained in the public service. Presently Dr. Wong is a consultant plastic surgeon at the Prince of Wales Hospital. He is also an honorary associate professor in both the University of Hong Kong and the Chinese University of Hong Kong, and an honorary consultant to the Department of Health, HKSAR. Dr. Wong has been on the committees of the Hong Kong Society of Plastic, Reconstructive and Aesthetic Surgeons, the Hong Kong Head & Neck Society, and the Hong Kong Burns Society. He has also been the secretary of the plastic surgery board of the Hong Kong College of Surgeons. Dr. Wong has published more than 40 peer reviewed scientific articles.

Dr. Wong has been interested in the law since early student days and has continued to use his spare time to read the law. In recent years, Dr. Wong has obtained the degrees of LLB (London), LLM (London) and the PCLL (HK).

Disclaimer

The author does not purport to represent that the views presented in this book are those of a lawyer providing legal advice. The text is only aimed at supplying the reader with general legal knowledge related to medical practice. The reader is strongly advised to seek proper legal advice in case of need.

The law as stated in this text is that of December 2009.

Preface

'The law is the law, is the law,' said Mrs Margaret Thatcher. That is how western liberal democratic societies view the rule of law. That spirit and upholding of the law as being above the human race, as a fundamental respect superior to man-made rules and regulations rather than taking the legal regime as a tool to govern people, is of supreme importance.

Given that the medical practitioner is of no real difference from the normal citizen in society in the eyes of the law, his activities are equally subject to its scrutiny. In fact, the law regards and accords a higher duty of standard to the doctor in his dealings with the patient. The simple reason quite obviously is that the relationship is one of a fiduciary kind with confidence entrusted to one party by the other and is of unequal arms' length. The law thus sees a need to intervene and offer a helping hand.

The modern medical practitioner is therefore not working in isolation. He is sanctioned in his duties to the patient. He needs both to be knowledgeable in his professional trade and to exercise a reasonable level of skill. He also should be versed in the relevant legal guidelines constantly being added to by the decisions and judgments given in the courts of law.

The doctor-patient context is an especially interesting one. The profession is constantly being 'watched' because medical activities have a large impact on the general public. Medical 'mishaps' always attract a great deal of attention in the media.

The main purpose of this work is to enable and empower the prudent medical practitioner in his daily work so that he can better understand what to do in the legal sense. It seeks to add confidence to the medical practitioner who is already well versed in his medical know-how. If the reader should additionally find his or her interest aroused by the diverse bits and pierces in the following pages, the author will have achieved his aim.

It is also hoped that the work will help the general reader to understand better the situation of their hard-working humble carers so that mutual understanding and respect can through bilateral participation and shared partnership enhance medical outcomes.

The approach taken in this work has been intentionally informal to avoid the boring, long-winded and technical presentation so often adopted in similar treatises. The aim is to stimulate thought and further inquiry rather to pretend to enrol exhaustive lists of alternatives and possibilities.

Opinions can and do differ. The opinions expressed in this book are entirely those of the author's. If you have your own views, the author is most pleased to know them. The author can be reached at: wsy2010a@hotmail.com.

I hope as readers you will find these pages inspiring and educational and will enjoy reading them.

David Sau-yan Wong
August 2010

List of Statutes

List of Cases

Introduction

It was the case when the author was a medical student that medical ethics teaching was neither included in the curriculum nor was there a subject as such. Nothing formal was ever mentioned in lectures or tutorials concerning the law in relation to medicine, with perhaps the one exception that abortion was legal under some circumstances. The only source of anything that could be considered ethics was actually from the student body itself – a huge poster on which was printed the words of the **Hippocratic Oath**. This was distributed free to every new medical freshman, although some proud classmates no doubt put it up in their rooms in hall for a collateral purpose, i.e. to remind themselves of that elitist feeling of a doctor-to-be.

In sharp contrast, legal education puts great emphasis on ethics teaching. **Professional Practice** is an important subject in the PCLL curriculum and it is taught in lectures supplemented with tutorials and case discussions, and is formally examined. No one can complete the course and become a lawyer without getting a pass in the subject.

It is, however, the case that in the past decade or so ethics has been given more and more emphasis and mention in most undergraduate as well as post-graduate medical refresher courses.

The issue is not whether one can practise, but whether given a licence to practise one can do so safely. Despite being armed with good medical knowledge and skills, it is perhaps still risky to be totally ignorant of the ethics and law in relation to one's practice. This is due to the increasingly litigious environment and the complicated procedures involved in medical practice.

The traditional coaching and apprenticeship nature of medical education is such that we learn from our predecessors' experience and unfortunate mistakes. This treatise is designed to provide a source of information from which medical practitioners, especially students and young doctors, can draw thought and, in the process, acquire a cautious and prudent attitude in their practice.

If the contents of this book do save any doctor from litigation, it will have been been worthwhile my writing it.

The following chapters are all independent and the reader is free to choose which to read first. I hope they arouse interest, inspire thought and stimulate questions.

Just a note on the search of Ordinances: the simplest way to look at the actual words of our Hong Kong Ordinances is to use the website of the **Hong Kong Legal Information Institute** (HKLII) at http://www.hklii.org, a contribution of the Faculty of Law of the University of Hong Kong to facilitate public access to the law.

A

The Hong Kong Legal System

1

The Hong Kong legal system – an overview

A very brief overview of the legal system in Hong Kong is presented here for the convenience of readers.

The **Basic Law** of the Hong Kong Special Administrative Region of the People's Republic of China (Chapter 2101 of the Laws of Hong Kong) was promulgated on 4 April 1990 and it took effect on 1 July 1997. The Basic Law functions as a constitution for the Hong Kong Special Administrative Region (HKSAR) but is not called as such because the HKSAR is a part of China and not an independent state.

The Basic Law stipulates that all the laws previously in force in Hong Kong are to be maintained, except for those that contravene the Basic Law and are subject to amendment by the HKSAR legislature.

What this means is that the **sources of the law** are the common law and the rules of equity, found in the judgments of the courts as precedents; the ordinances, referring to laws enacted in the statutes; subordinate legislation, which is delegated legislation usually dealing with specific issues; and some customary laws, representing certain Chinese traditional customs and rights which were practised and were recognised by the former British rule. Annex III of the Basic Law provides for those national laws of the People's Republic of China which apply in the HKSAR and these mainly relate to defence and foreign affairs. International conventions to which the HKSAR is a signatory have influential persuasive effects on the interpretation of the law until such times as they are enacted into domestic law and become directly enforceable.

The practical significance of the above is that we need to look at statutes as well as court decisions to understand what the law is. It is the typical feature of a common law system that judicial **interpretation of the law** is of immense importance. Only by reading actual judgments can one learn the true construction and meaning of many provisions as they appear in black and white. Ordinarily, the literal rule, i.e. the plain meaning of the words, is taken. When such an approach results in absurdity, the golden rule is used and that meaning is taken where the context dictates. The mischief rule occasionally employed looks at the defect of the common law before the existence of an ordinance to determine the purpose or reason for that ordinance so as to define the real meaning or intention behind the words. There is a trend in recent years towards a more purposeful approach in the interpretation of the law.

Where are the judgments found then? Past judgments are printed in '**Law Reports**'. These are somewhat akin to journals but are solely dedicated to judgments. Not all judgments are reported. Only those of the higher courts which are of value in terms of either the public interest or interpretation on points of law are reported usually. Nowadays the search of the law in past judgments is done almost exclusively through the computer via online databases.

Principles of law enunciated in past judgments as precedents are not limited to those from Hong Kong itself. In fact, most of the common law was derived from several hundred years of accumulated judgments and reports from England and this wealth of collection continues to be the common law today. In recent years, more and more we are seeing the common law of other commonwealth countries being cited, and with globalisation, even the laws of the United States and the European Union are often quoted.

In approaching a legal issue, it is first of all important to distinguish whether it is a criminal or a civil process that is involved.

Criminal prosecutions are almost always within the sphere of responsibility of the Department of Justice. The Secretary for Justice represents the HKSAR in its prosecutions against accused offenders and the standard of proof is beyond reasonable doubt. Criminal proceedings are usually brought with a view to punish law-breaking individuals or corporate bodies.

Civil proceedings, on the other hand, are usually instituted by one party against another party, be it an individual or a corporate. The standard required is lower and is based on the balance of probabilities. There are many different branches of the law that fall under this heading. The more important ones include contract, tort, land, property rights, administrative, family, revenue and probate. Civil proceedings are usually brought in order to enforce obligations or to seek a remedy when one's rights are infringed.

It is also important to remember that **the law is never static**. Court decisions, though obeying the **doctrine of judicial precedent**, change with the times and the values of society, usually by small incremental steps. That is the way the common law evolves. Statutory law undergoes revisions with time and sometimes whole statutes are repealed and new ones are written in their place. New legislation is made when the need arises. Bills are often introduced by legislative members or the Government itself. They are then subject to a process called the three readings and are studied by special committees formed for the purpose of any particular bill. Those bills that survive the third reading will eventually become law.

We have a **Law Reform Commission**, which is an advisory body which looks into areas where the law requires reform or where new law needs to be introduced. Its studies are presented in the form of reports to the Government and are made available to the public.

Legal practitioners are either solicitors or barristers. Solicitors are those whom lay clients turn to for legal services and are often known to be working in lawyers' firms, but they can also be in-house in institutions as advisors. They have a more limited right of audience than barristers who enjoy an unlimited right in all courts. Barristers do not serve lay clients directly but are instructed via a solicitor or a firm as the professional client. Barristers are particularly trained in arguing points of the law in the court. They are usually referred to as counsel in court, and very experienced barristers take silk and become senior counsels.

The **court system** is a hierarchical arrangement with the Court of Final Appeal at the highest, and then the High Court constituting both the Court of Appeal and the Court of First Instance. Under these are the District Court and the Magistrates' Courts. Other institutions in the system are the Coroner's Court and a number of tribunals dealing with specific areas defined by the law. The exact court in the system involved in any particular case depends upon a number of factors such as the nature of the proceeding, the weight of the offence or the amount of money involved in a claim, and the limitations in the jurisdiction and sentencing power of a particular court. The court system is operated by the Hong Kong Judiciary headed by the Chief Justice.

The **court process** can be very complicated to the outsider or novice. Essentially a trial consists of firstly an opening address either by the prosecution or the plaintiff depending on the nature of the case. This is followed by the tendering of exhibits, bundles and admitted facts. Witnesses are then called for an examination-in-chief by the prosecution or plaintiff. A defence lawyer then performs the cross-examination. The prosecution or plaintiff next re-examines the witnesses if necessary. The trial judge then may ask the witnesses questions. The prosecution or plaintiff then closes its case. If there is a case to answer, the above is repeated by the defence with its own witnesses. After that is over, the prosecution or plaintiff and then the defence respectively close their cases. The trial judge then sums up and the prosecution or plaintiff may make submissions following that. Thus far it is the elicitation of facts and evidence. The points of the law, if any, are now argued. The next step is the delivery of the judgment or verdict by the judge, or the jury if present. Sometimes this is delayed pending further deliberation by the judge or jury.

In criminal cases, the **sentencing** stage starts with the plea in mitigation by the legal representative of the convicted. Sentencing may be delayed awaiting the assessment reports of experts as required by the court, such as psychological assessment, home situation and background of the convicted, to enable it to arrive at the most suitable penalty. The judge then delivers the sentence taking into account the guilty plea if there was one, mitigation and aggravating factors.

The judge will also make a decision as to **costs** to be borne. These costs include expenses made in relation to the preparation of the case for trial. Often costs follow the event, meaning that the winning side can obtain costs from the losing side, but there are exceptions and the details are very complicated.

Both in criminal and civil proceedings, it is not to be forgotten that there is a complex procedural cascade of **stages before an actual trial**. In the case of a civil proceeding, this starts with the commencement of proceedings such as the issue of a writ, then the service of process, and the preparation of statement of claims and affirmations. There are often interlocutory applications like discovery of evidence and the making of interrogatories. Further complications to the layman are the making of sanctioned offers and payments. Needless to say, preparation of witness statements and affirmations are necessary before trial actually starts. In addition, even with a judgment order after trial a successful litigant sometimes may still need to resort to the court again for enforcement procedures.

For a criminal case, the details of procedure depend on the court in which the case is heard. No further discussion is made here as medical practitioners are less likely to be concerned by criminal prosecutions in their daily practice.

Whether as a plaintiff or a defendant, there is no strict rule in law to be represented. One can always appear in person, although that may not be wise in view of the complexity of the law and its procedures. In Hong Kong, we respect the **right to silence** and the **burden of proof** is always on the prosecution or the plaintiff. There is always a **presumption of innocence** until proven otherwise.

Laws can be substantive or procedural. Both can be very complex and a mistake or oversight in either can mean a lost battle in the adversarial process. **Substantive law** used to be the emphasis in the undergraduate curriculum while **procedural law** was reserved for the postgraduate legal practice course that is a requirement for eventual legal practice. There has been a tendency recently to intermingle the teachings in these disciplines for a more integrated approach.

The **Department of Justice** headed by the Secretary for Justice is responsible for prosecution in criminal matters as stated above. It also provides legal advice to the Government and drafts the law in additional to other important functions.

The **Legal Aid Department** is a Government-funded body established to provide legal assistance to people without the means to otherwise get assistance. The set criteria and levels of means for provision of legal aid can potentially be a barrier to 'justice for all', particularly with respect to that sector of the society which has exceeded the requirements but is yet too impoverished to have private legal representation. This 'sandwich class' may now qualify to apply for assistance under the Supplementary Legal Aid Scheme, which covers personal injuries and professional negligence cases where the amount of the claim exceeds HK$60,000.

It is not always the case that disputes have to be resolved in the courts. The court process is often lengthy, stressful and expensive. Neither do the courts encourage litigation. The modern trend worldwide is to promote **alternative dispute resolution**. This latter can be in the form of arbitration, mediation, or conciliation. Arbitration is the use of a third party as the 'judge', usually a mutually agreed relevant expert panel, and is an arrangement largely designed to stay outside the court system. Arbitration is more often employed in the settlement of industrial or commercial disputes. Mediation means the intervention of a middleman to help the opposing parties to reach a compromise. There is a growing scope for the use of mediation in personal injuries claims in recent years locally, and this is anticipated to increase further following the coming into effect in April 2009 of the Civil Justice Reform. In conciliation, the mediation process is carried further and the mediator suggests solutions to encourage a settlement. In real practice, an overwhelming majority of civil claims are settled by the parties at some stage before the actual trial.

References and Further Reading

1. *The Legal System in Hong Kong.* Department of Justice HKSAR 2004.
2. Albert Chen. *Legal System of the People's Republic of China*, 3rd edn. LexisNexis Butterworths 2004.
3. *Britain's Legal Systems.* Aspects of Britain series. HMSO 1996.
4. Mauet Thomas, McCrimmon Les. *Fundamentals of Trial Techniques.* Law Book Co of Australasia 2000.

B

Legal Issues

I

Medical Practice

2

What is fiduciary relationship?

In medical school, we doctors learnt about the **doctor-patient relationship**. In law, this relationship is classified under the special category of relationship known as fiduciary relationship. It is of paramount importance to understand what a fiduciary relationship means because that imposes special obligations on the doctor.

A **fiduciary relationship** exists when one party of the relationship places trust in the other party so that the latter has influence over the first party. Such a relationship therefore also exists between a solicitor and his client, a parent and child, a trustee and beneficiary, and a principal and agent.

In the presence of such a relationship, presumed **undue influence** may be said to have occurred if a patient goes into an agreement manifestly disadvantageous to himself. An example would be a terminal patient agreeing to pay medical fees of an amount extraordinarily huge and not in concordance with normally accepted practice.

The **obligations of a fiduciary relationship** are classically three, and in the context of the doctor and his patient:

- To act in a bona fide manner – In good faith for the benefit of the patient, e.g. not to influence your patient to undergo a second-best procedure because you need information to feed your research.
- To exercise powers properly – For the proper purpose, e.g. giving priority to a patient waiting for surgery other than for reason of urgency.
- To avoid a conflict of interests and not to profit from the superior position – Monetary reward should come second

to the patient's interests, e.g. ordering investigations for the sake of generating returns instead of indications.

It goes without saying that the above are additional to the basic duties of a doctor to a proper exercise of care, skill and due diligence; they are 'further and not in the alternative'.

Strictly speaking, it is not correct to regard the above as the court's imposition of extra burden on the medical profession. It is the high regard society has generously given to us and the reputation and entrustment we enjoy that require us to be vigilant in observing a higher standard of obligation.

References and Further Reading

1. Richard Edwards, Nigel Stockwell. *Trusts and Equity*, 5th edn. Longman 2002; pp 248-251.
2. Catherine Elliott, Frances Quinn. *Contract Law*, 3rd edn. Longman 2001; pp 181-184.
3. Paul Davies. *Gower and Davies' Principles of Modern Company Law*, 7th edn. Sweet & Maxwell 2003; pp 381-396, 421-424.

3

The professional duty of care

A **duty of care** means a legal obligation imposed on an individual to maintain a reasonable standard of care while performing acts that could cause foreseeable harm to another.

Such a duty serves in the law of tort to define the interests protected and whether a loss is actionable.

It may be of interest to briefly describe the origin of the concept of duty of care. This was in the landmark case of *Donoghue v Stevenson* (1932) where one Mrs. Donoghue fell ill after drinking half a bottle of ginger beer. The remains of a dead snail were then noticed to be present in the liquid still in bottle. The House of Lords found that the manufacturer owed a duty of care to Mrs. Donoghue. Lord Atkin propounded the '**neighbour principle**' that 'you must take reasonable care to avoid acts or omissions which you can reasonably foresee would be likely to injure your neighbour'. The word 'neighbour' is taken to mean anyone likely to be affected by one's activities.

The existence of a duty of care is onerous and the courts are always very careful before defining a new category of duty and so creating increasing causes of liability. Tests which the courts go through in this deliberation include the foreseeability of damage, legal proximity, and the 'just and reasonable' requirement.

For the medical practitioner, it is **trite law** to say that the doctor-patient relationship is inherently a specific duty situation. Apparently, this is a result of the considerable imbalance in arm's length in terms of medical knowledge between the doctor and the conventional patient, who is resting the fate of his or her body entirely on the decision of the medical expert. This means that if a doctor causes damage to his or her patient as a result of negligence, the patient would be entitled to bring an action for damages.

A duty of care arises from the moment when a doctor-patient relationship is started. Basically this means that the medical practitioner **formally and voluntarily assumes responsibility** for the care of the particular patient. Such a context may be the familiar scenario of a new patient entering the consultation room to seek treatment.

In this connection, a quotation from the judgment of the (English) Court of Criminal Appeal in *R v Bateman* (1927) is illustrative:

> 'If a person holds himself out as possessing special skill and knowledge and he is consulted, as possessing such skill and knowledge, by or on behalf of a patient, he owes a duty to the patient to use due caution in undertaking the treatment. If he accepts the responsibility and undertakes the treatment and the patient submits to his direction and treatment accordingly, he owes a duty to the patient to use diligence, care, knowledge, skill and caution in administering the treatment. No contractual relation is necessary, nor is it necessary that the service be rendered for reward.'

That case concerned a doctor who was involved in the difficult delivery of a baby. The baby ended up as a stillborn and the mother also died a week later, allegedly due to his negligence.

It is to be noted that a duty of care can also be established in the absence of an initiation by or approach from the patient. A doctor in the context of a rescuer, Good Samaritan or volunteer will thus potentially assume liability for negligence. In the Australian case of *Goode v Nash* (1979), a doctor who in a voluntary glaucoma screening exercise injured a patient's eye by accident was ordered to pay damages. Similarly, a medical practitioner who stops on the road to help a car accident victim will automatically assume a duty to exercise reasonable care.

Sometimes a duty can arise secondarily through the mediation of a third party. Typical examples are the examination of patients referred from insurance companies or of potential employees of an organisation.

There is a primary duty of care owed by the medical doctor in such circumstances to the referring party. Although a **secondary duty** is also owed to the person being examined, this is different from the normal doctor-patient relationship duty in that it merely requires causing no damage in the course of that examination or assessment, *X Minors v Bedfordshire County Council* (1995).

In contrast, no doctor-patient relationship generally means no duty of care. Thus, if a doctor receives a junk e-mail from a stranger seeking medical advice, he may chose not to reply to avoid establishing a doctor-patient relationship.

Once a duty exists, it continues to exist so long as the patient has not clearly indicated his wish not to continue to receive the care so as to put a termination to the relationship. In particular, the duty has no day and night relationship nor is it dependent on the doctor's duty hours. The corollary from this is that the doctor in charge should make proper arrangements to have his duties covered by colleagues when he is not available.

References and Further Reading

1. Suresh Nair. *Medical negligence: duty of care.* Singapore Medical Association News. July 2001; 33(7): 4-5.
2. Diana Kloss. *The duty of care: medical negligence.* Brit Med J 1984; 289: 66-68.
3. *Donoghue v Stevenson* (1932) AC 562.
4. *X Minors v Bedfordshire County Council* (1995) 3 WLR 152.
5. *R v Bateman* (1927) 19 Cr App R 8.
6. *Goode v Nash* (1979) 21 SASR 419.

4

What standard of care do doctors owe patients?

An awareness of the standard duty of care owed by doctors to patients is relevant because that is what the court uses as the gauge to measure whether we are discharging our duties properly.

What is required is the degree of competence usually to be expected of an **ordinary skilled member** of the profession. This is the reason why following usual practice is often regarded as a safe course of action.

What, then, if there are differences of opinion as to what is the best practice? This issue was addressed in 1957 in the English decision in *Bolam v Friern Barnet Hospital Management Committee*. The court said that a doctor would not be negligent if he had acted in accordance with 'a **practice accepted as proper** by a responsible body of medical men skilled in that particular art'. Therefore, on this judgment, quite simply if you can get someone authoritative to stand up in court to speak for you indicating that his view concurs with yours, the plaintiff would have a difficult time to prove that you are negligent.

The reader who is clear thinking will at this point have immediately realised that that decision has in reality left the standard to be defined by the medical profession. This seems to be perfectly logical and rational, but it would also mean that it is quite impossible to prove a doctor's negligence so long as there is some expert on his side.

The shortfall was thus remedied by the House of Lords decision in *Bolitho v City & Hackney Health Authority* in 1977. The court, while agreeing with *Bolam*, stated that it was not obliged to hold a doctor not negligent simply because some medical expert had testified that the doctor's actions were in line with some accepted practice. The courts were to take into account also the **reasonableness of the expert's opinion** and whether that has adequately weighed up the risks and benefits.

An excellent illustration of the above principles can be found in the case of *Marriott v West Midlands Regional Health Authority* (1999). A gentleman suffered a 'minor' head injury and was discharged home after overnight observation in hospital. He remained somewhat unwell for a week and called his family doctor, who found nothing was wrong and thus asked that the patient should return if he continued to feel unwell. Four days later, the patient became partially paralysed and this turned out to be related to the original injury. The family doctor was able to find an expert to support his opinion that no action was initially indicated due to the vagueness of the symptoms. The court applied *Bolitho* and considered the discretion not to take action was unreasonable in the circumstances.

What is the relevance of a doctor's experience in the formulation of a standard of care? There is no requirement for outstanding performance, just the skill of 'an ordinary member **in the position of the defendant'**. A junior doctor is not expected therefore to have the same level of skill as that of a consultant but only that of a reasonable junior doctor in his position, though irrespective of whether he is new. Thus, a medical officer working in a small rehabilitation home may be expected to have a standard different from that of his counterpart in a busy university hospital.

What about a doctor's knowledge of **new medical advances**? New developments in medical research certainly do change the standard of care expected of doctors. Failure to implement changes of practice due to a failure to look into new developments is negligence. Failure to implement changes after looking into new developments is also negligence.

An interesting example in this regard is provided by the case of *Roe v Minister of Health* (1954). A claimant paralysed after spinal anaesthesia failed in his claim because it was not medical knowledge at the time that storing ampoules of Nupercaine in phenol would allow percolation of phenol through micro-cracks in the ampoules. The court commented that with current knowledge it would be negligence not to realise the danger, but it was not then. The standard to be used by the court is therefore that which was current when the incident occurred.

References and Further Reading

1. *Bolam v Friern Barnet Hospital Management Committee* (1957) 2 All ER 118.
2. *Bolitho v City & Hackney Health Authority* (1977) 4 All ER 771.
3. *Marriott v West Midlands Regional Health Authority* (1999) Lloyd's Rep Med 23.
4. *Roe v Minister of Health* (1954) 2 QB 66.

5

Establishing a 'doctor-patient relationship' – the significance

Not infrequently doctors find themselves among friends and relatives on **social occasions** such as at family gatherings and dinner parties. In this situation, they are often bombarded with questions about health and for medical advice, which can not only prevent them from fully enjoying the event but also at times makes it difficult for them to deal with the questioning properly.

The problem underlying casual advice of this sort lies in its consequence should any damage result and the advice seeker then decide to pursue for liability.

Should a doctor on such occasions keep silent for peace of mind? Is it necessary to do so? How would the law look at this?

To understand the issue, it is important to realise that any claim for negligence will lie only where there is an **established doctor-patient relationship**. The rationale is easy to grasp. No liability, for example, will lie where a reporter pops up in your clinic and after asking a few questions, disappears and never shows up again. No relationship had formed and no duty of care exists. The question thus boils down to whether a doctor-patient relationship is established as a result of enquiries at social occasions and giving casual answers.

The strict answer is no because such 'consultations' are well understood to be informal and therefore not meant to be of any binding effect in the legal sense. They constitute **preliminary enquiries** possibly leading to a proper consultation and are not in themselves per se the consultation. The exchange of opinions is a matter of friendly communication and not the giving of professional advice. There has been no formal full history-taking or physical examination performed nor investigations done.

The doctor should therefore be safe from liability.

On the other hand, it has to be remembered that all depends on whether the above arguments are valid. In other words, it would have to do with whether the manner of the interaction is really a casual social exchange of ideas. It is therefore suggested that the prudent medical practitioner be reserved in his dealings in such circumstances. It cannot be wrong to advise the enquirer to make an appointment for consultation and be properly advised.

6

Delegation of duties

When more senior doctors become too busy to take up everything under them, or when they exercise their leadership and wish to confer a certain degree of autonomy for their team members' development, or simply when it is more appropriate, they delegate their duties. This is common practice.

What is relevant here is the liability issue when duties are delegated. Thus, for example, when one of your staff has ended up not doing a job properly, would you be in trouble or just the staff member because he or she is the person whose performance is in question not yours?

The legal perspective in this context will be analysed using the agency concept. **Agency** is not complicated in theory and is very helpful in this analysis.

An agent is an intermediary of the principal. He may have the express **authority** of the latter, or the authority may be implied, as when the agent is asked to do something which necessitated the authority from the principal. Authority may also be apparent or ostensible. This is when past dealings with third parties give rise to a reasonable belief that the agent has authority.

With any of these three authorities, the **principal** is bound and will be liable for the agent's dealings and actions. Both the agent and the principal are liable and the third party may choose from which one of them, or both, to claim in established damages.

When would an agent be solely liable personally? He would be if the principal is undisclosed so that the third party believed that he was dealing with the agent alone. Of course, if the 'agent' proceeded without any authority at all, he would be liable himself for warranty of authority.

There is one more point. When one delegates, it is vital and essential to select someone with the required **competence** to do the concerned job. It goes without saying that should the agent in such a scenario be unable to produce an acceptable result, the principal remains liable.

From the point of view of the person delegated a duty, he should confirm authority from his principal, perhaps on each critical occasion or step. It is paramount that he stays within his given powers and ensures that his competency is sufficient. In the event of any doubt, further advice and instructions should be sought from the principal.

References and Further Reading
1.   Elliott C, Quinn Q. *Contract Law*, 3rd edn. Longman 2001; pp 199-201.
2.   *Good Medical Practice*. General Medical Council 2006. Paragraphs 41-55. Available on the web at http://www.gmc-uk.org/guidance/good_medical_practice.

7

Registration – the meaning

It might be better to present this topic in the form of questions and answers.

Q: How can one **lawfully practise medicine** in Hong Kong?

A: Be a registered medical practitioner, i.e. obtain a licence to practise medicine.

Q: Why do we need to get registered if we already have a medical degree?

A: A medical qualification or degree from a university is merely evidence of medical education, not a licence to practise medicine.

Q: What penalty is there to **practise without registration**?

A: Potentially imprisonment for up to 5 years, and if resulting in personal injuries, up to 7 years.

Q: What about **fraudulent registration**?

A: Potentially imprisonment for up to 5 years.

Q: Is simple registration per se sufficient?

A: Registration, if accepted, would result in the issue of a licence to practise medicine. In addition to this, a valid practising certificate is required under section 20A of the Medical Registration Ordinance, Chapter 161 of the Laws of Hong Kong. This practising certificate has to be renewed annually by application subject to a fee and submission of no conviction in the form of a declaration (section 5 of the Medical Registration (Miscellaneous Provisions) Regulations, Chapter 161 of the Laws of Hong Kong).

Q: Who takes care of registration?
A: The Medical Council of Hong Kong.

Q: Who is to seek **Limited Registration**?
A: Limited registration is for the purpose of employment of a medical practitioner who is only registered outside Hong Kong, of good character, with approved overseas qualifications and with the relevant experience.

Q: Is there **exemption** from registration?
A: Under section 29 of the Medical Registration Ordinance, medical officers of Her Majesty's Forces serving on full pay in Hong Kong, or ships' surgeons while in the discharge of their duties, are exempted.

Q: What about **Provisional Registration**?
A: This applies to practitioners who have passed the qualifying degree examination or the licentiate examination and is for the purpose of their initial employment.

Q: Is registration always linked to **licence to practise**?
A: Not necessarily. In the United Kingdom, a proposed change in the regulation of the medical profession is that the two will be delinked. A medical practitioner will need to be both registered and to obtain a licence to practise. The latter will require revalidation meaning demonstration of practice of a standard up to that prescribed by the General Medical Council. The purpose of the delinkage is apparently an

attempt to enforce continuing professional development and to ensure fitness to practise.

References and Further Reading

1. Medical Registration Ordinance, Chapter 161 of the Laws of Hong Kong.
2. Medical Registration (Miscellaneous Provisions) Regulations, Chapter 161 of the Laws of Hong Kong.
3. The website of the Hong Kong Medical Council at http://www.mchk.org.hk/doctor/index.htm.

8

What to include on your name card

It is quite well known that there are restrictions on what degrees are quotable on a name card. Who decides this? What is the purpose of doing so?

The source of this restriction is found in Ref MC 8/E of paragraph B (Communication in Professional Practice) in Part II of the 'Code of Professional Conduct' promulgated by the Medical Council of Hong Kong. The **List of Quotable Qualifications** is constantly being updated upon applications received for inclusion and deliberation by the Education and Accreditation Committee. The List consists of qualifications which are allowed to be quoted on name cards, letter heads and sign boards. There is no express reference to those qualifications which are not on the List and so presumably they are not quotable by inference, unless an application has been made to the Council and then considered suitable to be added to the List.

The interesting question is when a doctor has further degrees and **qualifications which are not medically related** and thus obviously not on the List but he wishes to include them on his name card, can he do so legitimately?

No express stipulation, unfortunately, could be found in official sources. The solution is therefore to be a matter of interpretation. This process is also incidentally an illustration of how lawyers approach problems.

The first clue is to look at the **intention** behind the List in order to see what interpretation is most appropriate. In the Revised Guidelines for Consideration of Quotable Qualifications released by the Medical Council which took effect from 1 April 2006, the purposes of the

Quotable List scheme and the factors that the Committee would take into consideration in its deliberation were explained. The objectives of the scheme were described as giving recognition to registrable basic and postgraduate medical education and to providing information as to further medical training for the public and for other medical practitioners when making referrals. It is therefore clear that the scheme is aiming at the regulation of medical degrees only.

The second line of approach is to resort to basic **common sense**. The Medical Council of Hong Kong is a statutory body functioning to regulate the medical profession. It is not empowered to make irrational decisions. What good reasons would there be for taking away the right of any ordinary person to quote authentic qualifications on his name card? The only justification is that medically related qualifications, if quoted, would and could be misleading if left uncontrolled, because there are bound to be risk takers putting down fake qualifications. It is widely known, not only within the medical profession, that there are organisations and bodies which issue certificates of membership simply upon the submission of a fee! That would, if left uncontrolled, lead to confusion both to the public as well as within our own profession.

Taking the above two approaches together, the conclusion must be that there should be nothing wrong in putting down your MSc, MBA, LLB, MA, MMus, or even MH, JP, GBS, MBG, etc.

References and Further Reading
1. The website of the Hong Kong Medical Council at http://www.mchk.org.hk/quotable.htm.

9

Notes in the charts as evidence of fact

Junior doctors are often reminded of the importance of **documentation** in the hospital charts. In some hospitals, there is regular auditing of signatures, dates and hours of orders, legibility, etc.

In addition to merely accurate record keeping, the hospital charts are potential **evidence of facts** in a litigation dispute. This might perhaps bring home the reminder that obsession with documentation is well warranted and rewarded. The reason is precisely that whatever is not written down was arguably not in the doctor's mind at the time the record was made! The medical practitioner thus assumes the burden of proving what he would like to assert against the opposing allegation of the claimant.

An obvious example would be something alleged not to have been mentioned as a caution in obtaining a patient's consent. Indeed, it would be highly reasonable for a claimant to say that the doctor would not have forgotten to put down that very something had he regarded it as important.

Clear and complete records are thus for mutual benefit. For patients, their care is guaranteed against misunderstandings against the carers as a result of omissions and incomplete documentation. For doctors, they are good **contemporaneous** evidence of what happened, which will be helpful in their defence against frivolous claimants.

As the notes are of such importance, they should be well preserved in case they need to be retrieved later for the purposes of complaints and litigations, and of course medical management. Theoretically, the longer patients' records are kept the better. There are policies with hospitals as to the length of time patients' records are kept from when they last received treatment. With modern computer technology it should now be feasible to keep records permanently.

10

Your signature

What is so magical about a signature? Why do we have to sign our orders and notes? Couldn't my colleagues recognise my hand-writing?

A signature is something of immense implication in the law. It is, in simple terms, your official verification of what lies above your signature in the same document. In other words, once signed, the person who signs approves of what is there. It is a **sign of endorsement**. There are therefore no grounds to go back and refute what was written or printed above the signature unless there is fraud or mistake. For the same reason, any subsequent alteration of what was written requires that to be cross-signed.

A personal chop carries the same significance.

Because of the legal implication of one's signature, any prudent person would take the greatest care before adding his or her signature and thus assuming responsibility and liability for anything.

A case in question is the usual practice of junior doctors being asked to sign a particular laboratory request form or a prescription sheet for another doctor just for convenience. This sometimes happens when the responsible intern is not around and another happens to be there. If anything goes wrong, the one who signs will be directly liable. It is therefore advisable to check carefully all details before signing or better to politely request that trouble be taken to get the proper person to put down his own signature.

It may be of interest to learn that in law there is a doctrine called ***non est factum***, meaning 'that is not my deed'. The basis of this is that there had been such a fundamental misunderstanding as to the nature of a document that the signature should not bind the one who signed it. In the English case of *Gallie v Lee* (1971), an elderly widow signed a document to transfer her house to a nephew. In fact, the document was a deed of sale to another called Lee but the old lady did not read it because she had broken her glasses. After her death, the administrator of her estate sought a declaration of *non est factum* to make the agreement with Lee void. The House of Lords refused. Lord Reid said: 'The plea cannot be available to anyone who was content to sign without taking the trouble to find out at least the general effect of the document.'

Indeed, authorities have cited the rarity, if ever, of this defence being successful in relieving liability from one's very own signature. The significance of a signature therefore needs no further emphasis.

References and Further Reading

1.   *Gallie v Lee* (1971) AC 1039.

11

Alteration of medical records

Medical notes are to medical practitioners a record of the patient's treatment for his management purpose. It allows the retrieval of information in this regard so that references can be made in the future when there is a need.

Incidentally, the medical notes are also an important source of information when there is a claim of liability against the medical treatment offered. The high importance accorded to the medical notes in law is due to the fact that they are a **contemporaneous documentation** of facts and opinion and are thus of high probative value as compared with recalls from memory months to years later of what had happened.

In other words, the law regards what is inside the medical record as reliable evidence in the absence of proof that it is not.

With such knowledge in mind, the medical practitioner should need no reminder to keep accurate and complete notes.

A guide to what is important and complete would be to include what one would suppose a reasonable person would think is relevant if the case should go to court.

The medical record, in this sense, is actually a document which speaks for the medical practitioner if he sensibly deals with it. On the contrary, sloppy medical notes could end up as evidence against the doctor when they are incomplete and poorly entered. What has or has not been mentioned is a ready and obvious example when obtaining consent for a procedure.

For obvious reasons, any subsequent or **retrospective alteration** of the medical notes recorded is best avoided. It is preferable to enter new notes following the previous notes rather than crossing out old notes or, even worse, making them illegible. Clearly crossing out inappropriate notes made is alright when done in a neat and tidy manner. Any note entry must be dated, timed and signed. If the alteration involves an agreement made with the patient, such as an explanation given for the purpose of obtaining consent, then the patient's counter-signature is also required. It might be better to sign another new form altogether to supersede the original if the alteration is not merely trivial.

Medical notes, to be of value both as a medical record as well as **evidence** in law, have to be kept safely and be retrievable when needed. The old-style filing done by a few clerks in a remote cell somewhere in the hospital compound has nowadays been replaced by large-scale modernised record keeping departments in most major hospitals, some of which are operating as efficiently as book libraries. This is often supplemented by computerised versions of the records, which are maintained by information technology supporting units.

12

What to include in the medical notes

This is a question of obvious relevance in our practice of medicine but is one to which we do not usually give a lot of attention.

Help in answering the question may be found in Part II Section A paragraph 1 of the Code of Professional Conduct of the Medical Council of Hong Kong, where details are provided about medical records.

In essence, the medical notes represent the documentation of a patient's medical management. For this purpose, they must be systematic, comprehensive, true, adequate, clear and contemporaneous. Notes have to be detailed enough to allow comprehension and continuity of care by colleagues.

Medical notes can be printed or written so long as they are legible.

For practical reasons, however, we do not, and it is not advisable to, put down each and every word uttered between the doctor and the patient. What should be included are the relevant and material points which record the salient positive and negative features of the patient's condition, progress, investigation results, the patient's requests and preferences, his/her consents or refusals with the given reasons, procedures and treatments offered, arrangements planned and justifications for any medical decisions.

Maintaining the quality of a medical record is a part of quality medical management and is also evidence of whether management provided is up to standard.

The contents of a medical record will reflect directly on the credibility of the practitioner's evidence in court. Many a time arguments presented by lawyers are based upon the absence of specific critical statements in the medical notes.

A simple way to tell whether any particular statement should be entered into the medical notes is to ask oneself if inclusion or exclusion of that statement would make a difference to colleagues learning about the case or when the record was read and interpreted by a third party such as a lawyer. If the answer is in the affirmative, it is obviously better to include that material.

References and Further Reading

1. Code of Professional Conduct of the Medical Council of Hong Kong, Part II Section A Paragraphs 1.1.1-1.1.4.

—— 13 ——

The chaperone

What is a chaperone?

In former times in western societies, an adult person often accompanied a young unmarried man or woman on social occasions in order to prevent inappropriate social or sexual interactions or illegal behaviour. This person was usually answerable to the parents of the accompanied. 'Chaperone' is derived figuratively from the French word 'chaperon', meaning 'hood', using the analogy of a hood covering a bird's head so that it looses its desire to fly away.

The word is thus borrowed in medical practice to refer to a third party to the doctor and the patient who acts as the neutral person **eye witness** in interactions between the doctor and patient, traditionally during examinations involving a male doctor and a female patient. A chaperone is thus a witness and safeguard for both parties during a medical examination or procedure. The chaperone ensures that the female patient is not molested and protects the male doctor from being falsely accused. Chaperones are therefore particularly important in gynaecological and other examinations of an intimate nature.

Who can be a chaperone? Theoretically any adult third person who is mentally sound is an acceptable candidate. The doctor's nurse is an obvious choice as she is on the spot and capable. Conventionally a female nurse was required because the point was primarily to protect the female patient.

In addition to being an eye witness, a chaperone can also provide the support patients often require during embarrassing or uncomfortable procedures or examinations.

The importance of having a chaperone is self-evident and the sensible medical practitioner is therefore advised to be absolutely strict with this practice. It goes without saying that because of the above, we should be thankful to the chaperone.

That is the classical teaching. One wonders whether with the more liberal attitudes of today towards sex and sexual inclination if it would be advisable for chaperones to be around even for the examination of male patients, and when female doctors examine women.

14

Treating friends and relatives

It may surprise the reader to know that there are medical practitioners who deliberately avoid treating friends and relatives. Indeed, this is not unique to the medical profession.

Many lawyers also avoid accepting their own relatives and friends as clients and prefer to refer them to reliable colleagues.

Judges are supposed to do justice and to be seen to be doing so and they will declare any possible hint of a **conflict of interest**. As a sideline, in the infamous UK *General Pinochet* case of 1998, even the House of Lords was forced to overturn its own ruling. This was as a result of Lord Hoffman having had an undeclared interest in Amnesty International, which was granted leave to intervene and make representations in the proceedings. Along the same vein, in *R v Sussex Justices ex p McCarthy* (1924), Lord Hewart laid down the well-known and often quoted words in the dictum of the case, that 'justice must not only be done but should manifestly and undoubtedly be seen to be done'. Judges should therefore not sit in a case in which they have an interest.

For medical practitioners, of course, there is nothing in the law against treating friends and relatives. However, it is not uncommon also to hear and encounter problems and complications particularly when one is treating this special category of patient. It is often said that VIPs are associated with bad luck. Some have even labelled the problems encountered the **VIP syndrome**.

Obviously there is no scientific basis for that statement. What it says, however, is nevertheless not entirely untrue. The problem here lies in the objectivity we exercise in our decisions. It is the emotional reaction, the affection, the concern and the anxiety, etc, that could encourage us to do something a little differently from the normal course we usually take under a particular set of circumstances. That is where the source of the problem arises.

The message is that if we cannot be totally impartial and free from **subjectivity**, it might be more appropriate to seek help from colleagues. On the other hand, if a doctor can be sure of his or her good judgment and decision, there is no rule of ethics or law to dictate otherwise. The author has personally come across a confident young surgeon repairing a hernia-hydrocele complex for his baby son in a most elegant manner.

References and Further Reading
1. *R v Bow Street Metropolitan Magistrates ex p Pinochet Ugarte, sub nom R v Evans, R v Bartle* (1998) 3 WLR 1456.
2. *R v Sussex Justices ex p McCarthy* (1924) 1 KB 256.
3. *Gallie v Lee* (1971) AC 1039.

15

Examining your colleague!

The author once overheard an interesting story from two colleagues who had practised in the United Kingdom for a number of years. Colleague A was flipping through a medical journal and was suddenly surprised at seeing the name of someone she knew as the author of an article. She explained that she had actually once worked with this doctor, a male, in the same unit. One evening when the doctor was on call, all was very quiet and peaceful. A young nurse, pretty and in her early twenties, was on duty with him; and in the middle of the night with little happening on the ward the nurse sought this (also young) male doctor's advice for discomfort in the chest. Accordingly he performed a physical examination of her to see if anything was wrong. It was said that he listened to the heart sounds and palpated her breasts. Unable to find anything wrong, he reassured her. The next day the nurse reported being **sexually assaulted**. Colleague B then made a comment, which may well have been flippant and the author assumes no liability for its authenticity, as it is hearsay. Colleague B said that this situation was not uncommon. The young male doctor's mistake was that he was too professional at the wrong thing: while he had been very professional in his examination and did just what the books taught him, he had been less than professional in dealing with a lady! Apparently the poor young male doctor eventually won his case.

The author has also personally heard 'rumours' of a similar case in a big regional hospital in Hong Kong. A nursing sister on a surgical unit sought advice from the consultant surgeon of the unit for a breast lump. He took her into his own office, closed the door, had her undressed and examined her without the presence of a third person. He might have been a very considerate doctor because in this situation one would naturally expect that the ward sister would want the privacy and confidentiality of the 'consultation' to be observed. The assumption unfortunately was wrong! The sister alleged indecent assault the following day.

The bring-home message is to allow **no concession**. Everyone deserves equal treatment in law as much as in medicine. Do what is necessary and omit nothing. Friends are to be respected but not unfairly treated!

A remark from my Colleague A raised another interesting point. Assuming sexual offences in medical situations are always committed by men towards women, he told the younger lady Colleague B that she'd be immune if he should seek her help for scrotal pain. That was obviously a joke, but the assumption is incorrect. Indecent assault in law can be towards a man as well as a woman. It can also be a man indecently assaulting another man. Take no risk. The reader may be surprised to learn that in the common law of some commonwealth jurisdictions, a woman is capable of raping a man as well as a woman!

16

Medical or professional insurance – is it necessary?

Insurance is a **sharing of risk**. If any practitioner is unfortunate enough to be sued and held responsible for damages, every subscribing member of the insurance society pays. The brunt of the damages is thus shared collectively.

Any doctor working on his own in an individual practice should be aware that such protection is valuable and advisable.

The issue with insurance arises when one is an employee, such as when working with the Hospital Authority, and whether having your own **individual professional insurance** is really necessary. Everyone knows that medical protection fees have escalated astronomically in recent years.

One argument is that if you are involved in a claim while in employment, the employer should be held **vicariously liable**. With an institution like the Hospital Authority, there is no reason why the claimant's lawyer would not give the advice to sue the institution so as to ensure that large damages are met.

In truth, an involved doctor is not, however, immune. He would be held **jointly and severally liable** to the claimant. This means that both the doctor and the institution are liable. The fact that the institution is vicariously liable does not to any extent reduce the doctor's liability. Severally means that the claimant is free to make his full claims against the concerned doctor(s) and/or the institution. Indeed, there are good reasons for the lawyer representing the institution to argue against any incrimination of negligence or other faults as being related to the course of employment, if possible, because the institution's interest is different from that of the doctor(s).

For this reason, it is surely necessary to insure oneself professionally for peace of mind.

An interesting question then is why such professional insurance schemes are instead called **indemnities**. The dictionary meaning of indemnity is cover, insurance, protection, compensation... etc. In law, the most important distinction of significance to the medical practitioner is that an indemnity society only offers the right to have your application considered. It retains full discretion as to whether to offer advice despite the fact that no term of the contract of indemnity is violated. With insurance, provided one is within the terms of the policy, one can sue the insurance company if one is turned down in a claim as a breach of contract..

One last thing that we should note is the term 'occurrence-based' as opposed to 'claims-based' where the nature of coverage is concerned. An '**occurrence-based**' policy responds to a claim in the past provided that at the occurrence of the event giving rise to the subsequent claim, the policy was open. This is of particular usefulness to the medical practitioner because it means doctors do not have to worry about the past upon retirement from practice or on a change of insurer. A '**claims-based**' scheme, on the other hand, would only compensate if the event and the actual claim are both made at a time when the policy is open.

References and Further Reading

1. Hodgin Ray. *Insurance Law: Text and Materials*, 2nd edn. Routledge-Cavendish 2002; Chapter 1 General introduction, pp 26-27.
2. Hodgin Ray. *Insurance Law: Text and Materials*, 2nd edn. Routledge-Cavendish 2002; Chapter 8 Claims, p 580.

17

Remote control medical orders

The author will illustrate what can happen with remote control medical orders with an incident from his own experience.

One quiet evening I was called by the first on-call doctor and advised that a patient who had sustained a burn injury was being admitted through the Accident and Emergency Department. The victim had suffered the injury 2 days earlier on the mainland and having been repatriated through the SOS system had just arrived. He had neither an intravenous line nor an endotracheal tube. Learning that this history was given over the phone, the reader may well agree that the patient was unlikely to be too seriously injured. Plastic surgeons prefer to avoid general intensive care units because they are often the areas in the hospital with the most well-selected resistant and virulent organisms. A decision was therefore made for the victim to be sent to the Burns Unit pending further assessment by myself as I was already on my way back to the hospital.

Ten minutes later, I was paged again and was informed that the victim was already on his way to the ICU because the junior intensive care doctor on duty was worried about the risk of airway involvement, particularly after resuscitation! To avoid confusing the reader, you would not be worried about airway oedema if your patient 48 hours after the burn had remained well without intubation. Furthermore, the dynamics of capillary permeability changes are such that fluid extravasation would not follow leakage of protein by the end of the first 24 hours.

What should I have done at that juncture? Overrule the decision to have the patient sent to the ICU or get to the hospital as quickly as possible to find out more first? I took the latter option.

The reason is simple. It is always dangerous to give **phone orders** even if you are very confident about things.

The context is particularly common for more junior doctors. Often they are paged by the wards in the middle of the night for little minor events and they are tired. The temptation to give orders without seeing the patient is often real.

From the legal point of view, this is a simple and straightforward **negligence** situation because no reasonable doctor would make a decision affecting a patient without even going to see what has happened. Professionally this is **unethical** behaviour because it is impossible to claim that one has exercised his best skill to care for the patient.

The author also wishes to cite another incident which he will never forget because it resulted in the saving of three lives. Three months after graduation I was doing my obstetrics rotation as a house officer in an obstetrics hospital. At 3am one winter morning I was called by the admission ward to see a pregnant primigravida patient with abdominal pain who had had no antenatal care thus far. The woman's pregnancy had reached 34 weeks' maturity and poor young me was, in those days, alone to examine this desperate patient with the aid of, at the most, a stethoscope, a table light microscope with a few re-used glass slides, test tubes, urine 'stix' and a proprietary kit for pregnancy testing. Of course, the most valuable resource to fall back on was: call your senior.

On seeing the patient, it was impressive that the pain being complained of was out of proportion to the minimal vaginal spotting. Furthermore, the size of the abdomen was much larger than one would have expected for a normal pregnancy of 34 weeks. The abdomen was also tense and fetal heart sounds were not heard. The blood pressure was stable.

After immediately escorting the patient to the ward, keeping her nil without food and water, and setting up the drip, the first on-call medical officer was paged. However, the answer was for me to settle the patient and that she would come later. After waiting for one whole hour and with the suspicion of an accidental haemorrhage in mind, I bravely went on to call the second on-call. The second on-call only answered the second attempt at paging 20 minutes after the first paging, which was unanswered, but said she had yet to see such a case and sleepily proclaimed that she had serious doubt about my diagnosis. Her basis was that she was very familiar with the books because she was about to sit the MRCOG in a month's time and was therefore very certain that I was wrong in view of the rarity of the condition! An authoritative but illogical deduction!

Not content with the response, I proceeded to call the third on-call doctor who was an Englishman and had been a consultant in England before he took up the post of senior lecturer in the university. He was a really professional doctor and a gentleman. He said he would return to the hospital immediately. By this time, it was already some 4 hours since the patient's admission, the morning light was just beginning to show its presence through the windows and my efforts were finally being met with some recognition. The Maw's test I had sent earlier by special arrangement with the mother teaching hospital was traced on the phone in anticipation of the boss's arrival: it was POSITIVE! The next minute the boss stepped into the ward. He ordered immediate transferral of the patient back to the teaching hospital and asked me to book and prepare for an emergency Caesarean section.

I subsequently learnt from classmates working in the teaching hospital that the whole department was in the theatre at the Caesar… and fortunately both mother and babies were well. It was indeed a twin pregnancy as I had strongly suspected.

What was the price for the good night's sleep? You can guess it, but that is the danger of making phone orders.

18

Medical consultation – urgent

It was, and unfortunately sometimes still is, the case that inter-disciplinary consultations in public hospitals are seen as something of secondary importance. Often only the most junior staff is deployed to be responsible and such consultations are of the lowest priority in one's list of duties. The result is that a minor problem is often the reason for prolonging a hospital stay by several additional days just waiting for another specialty to see the patient before discharge.

This should not and need not be the norm.

For one specific reason, the author always sees cases as soon as possible whether urgent or not if they should come into his hands. This is because liability is assumed the moment the doctor is imparted with the knowledge and thus '**put on enquiry**'. There is no excuse for any delay should the patient's condition change in the interim once the doctor has been informed. Why, then, is it sensible to wait?

A case in hand but not yet seen is thus a time bomb waiting to explode. Although it may not do so, if it does go off the doctor will be injured also, not just the patient.

It is perhaps not so much that doctors are too busy but rather the relative importance they ascribe to various activities. Do not let something which you regard as of less importance to develop into something which will overwhelm you with unnecessary trouble.

19

Checking laboratory results

In his early days as a freshman to the great profession, the author was taught: 'Do not order any blood if you don't go back to look at the results.'

This was a remark made by an experienced senior colleague who found a deranged blood coagulation result filed in a patient's notes without any action having being taken after an on-call night. In fact, it had come to the attention of no one! Whose responsibility was it to look for it? In that situation, it had to be the on-call doctor who asked for the blood. If the results were not back before his shift was over, it was his duty to pass the responsibility on to the next doctor on call.

However, one might question whether this doctrine proffered by the senior doctor is correct. It appears to be an eternal truth but the author tends to think that the decision to check blood should not be dictated by whether one would be around to see the results. The ultimate criterion should always be whether the investigation is indicated in the circumstances.

A better version of the message may thus have been: 'Always check the results of your investigations.'

This is another real story again. A gentleman fell from a ladder while attempting to change a ceiling light bulb in his home. He was admitted briefly for a minor head injury. He was observed and appeared well. At follow-up, he reported to the doctor that he had been sexually incompetent since the fall! The doctor somehow took blood for a prolactin level. The patient never returned. The prolactin level was sky high and was in a range diagnostic of a prolactinoma, but it came to the notice of nobody. Five years later, the gentleman was investigated by another doctor for headache and subsequent investigations revealed a pituitary tumour. By then, there was already irreversible visual impairment.

Would the first doctor be liable? Had his duty of care finished, with a blood ordered by him, and thus considered relevant by him, without reading it?

No matter where you might regard the error to be, liability in terms of **negligence** is obvious.

It is also worth emphasising that one should always read the results of one's investigations in a timely manner. The liability of any delay resulting thereby in damage is also assumed by the attending doctor.

20

Phoned laboratory reports

This is a tricky area that is easily overlooked.

Phone-reports can be made by the laboratory for a number of reasons. The test could be urgent and the laboratory is keen to let the clinician know the result. The result may be very abnormal and urgent action is expected. The request may be intra-operative such as a frozen section examination required for immediate decision-making. In any case, the results of phone-reports are likely to be of more than usual importance often calling for instant action.

The obvious risk inherent in verbal phone-reports is of course **misunderstanding**.

Whatever the reason for the phone-report, it is thus of vital importance that the report is accurately relayed. This includes the identity of the patient concerned, the result itself, the name of the staff communicating the result, and the nature, date and time of the test. It might be worthwhile to double-confirm on the spot by repeating what is heard and said. Documentation is obviously a must. It is better also to request a fax copy of the result immediately after the communication for verification.

It does not need saying that a mistake can potentially result in a disastrous outcome. It is the practice of many laboratories to issue a fax copy immediately following the verbal phone-report on a routine basis.

A mistake made in the communication of results causing damage to patients can be grounds for a claim of negligence.

21

Dress codes: skirt and tie

Gone are the days when male doctors were seen being stared at and scolded by grand authoritative professors in hospital corridors for not wearing ties and female doctors for not being in skirts at work. This was actually not such a distant past and was the dress-code norm when the author was a medical student in the late 70s and early 80s.

No doubt the underlying rationale for such restrictions was related to the **image and prestige** of the profession in the eyes of the public. Whether the profession now enjoys as much esteem as it used to is not the purpose of the present discussion.

It is, however, a fact of life nowadays that the tradition is no longer maintained. Many young male colleagues run about from ward to ward in trainers and a lot of female doctors wear trousers to work. Even some very senior lady doctors actually do the same both in the hospital setting as well as when attending important ceremonies and events of a professional nature.

One amusing personal experience the author had concerns an 'old-fashioned' examiner who enjoyed a very influential position in his specialty. He commented to the rest of the examiners in a pre-examination preparation meeting that he had been very unhappy with lady doctor X who had never been seen wearing a skirt to work. He warned that should Doctor X come to the viva in trousers, he would fail her for that reason alone. It transpired that the signal was 'picked up' in time by lady doctor X, who turned up in a smart skirt, although unfortunately she was still held back by difficult questions.

Let us elaborate on the issue of lady doctors not wearing skirts. Is there any protection or recourse in the law if you were faced with a situation where a strict boss required you as a lady doctor to wear a skirt? What might help you? Could there be a case for **discrimination** under the Sex Discrimination Ordinance?

Dress code is not an area specifically addressed in the Ordinance but over the years the courts have formulated principles for dealing with cases where people have felt that they are being discriminated against compared with the other sex when it comes to appearance. Is it a viable claim that since men have the right to wear trousers, and if only women are 'forced' to put on skirts, it is a discrimination based on one's sex?

The principles that have emerged as a result of the common law are that:

- Merely treating men and women differently does not necessarily mean unlawful discrimination, unless one sex suffers a detriment. Wearing a tie or a skirt is not a detriment.

- Provided men and women are both required to maintain similar standards of smartness according to '**conventionality**', no discrimination can be held. It is thus lawful, for example, to require men to have short hair while permitting women long hair. Similarly, it is permissible to require men to wear conventional business suits while permitting women more freedom in their dress.

In *Smith v Safeway plc* (1996), Mr. Smith was dismissed because his pony tail grew too long to be kept under his work hat. The English Court of Appeal noted that the employers were seeking to promote a 'conventional' image. Lord Justice Phillips said: 'An **appearance code** which applies a standard of what is conventional to both men and women is one which is even-handed between men and women and not discriminatory.' The court also added that: 'Discrimination consists not in failing to treat men and women the same, but in treating those of one sex less favourably than those of the other.'

A specific example concerning skirts is the case of *Schmidt v Austicks Bookshops* (1977). Ms. Schmidt, who worked in a bookshop, was not allowed to wear trousers at work. The court laid down the principle that so long as both sexes were subject to restrictions in how they presented themselves, albeit not the same restrictions, given the difference between men and women there would be no discrimination.

It would seem therefore that discrimination principles would not come to a lady's help on the issue of being forced to wear skirts.

Another recent interesting example concerned a British Airways employee who lost her fight to openly wear a cross on a chain at work at Heathrow. The employee's contention was one of freedom of expression of one's faith. The employer's case was its uniform policy so that such items could only be worn if concealed underneath the uniform. The argument got heated coverage in the press and even Members of Parliament expressed their concern. The case has not proceeded to the court at the time of writing and it will be very interesting to see, if it was to do so, how the court would analyse the matter. The crucial point is likely to lie in whether it would consider that the wearing of turbans and hijabs, which was allowed by the employer, constitutes a discriminatory element. There may be difficulties in basing an argument on racial discrimination because wearing a cross is not race specific nor is the wearing of a turban or a hijab. It may, however, be possible to resort to one based upon religion because there may be grounds under section 3(1)(b) of the (English) Employment Equality (Religion or Belief) Regulations 2003 (No. 1660), in terms of indirect discrimination. An indirect discrimination in this context is where a practice of an employer impacts adversely on certain employees because of their religion. Indirect discrimination can be justified if there is an objective business reason that is appropriate and necessary and it will remain to be seen if British Airways can convince the court of the existence of such.

The author's personal view is that there are good reasons for conventional dress codes. It would seem that it is preferable for members of the medical profession to continue to present a respectable image to patients. If we are well-disciplined individuals, we should be well disciplined from inside out as well as from the outside in!

References and Further Reading

1.   Sex Discrimination Ordinance, Chapter 480 of the Laws of Hong Kong.
2.   (English) Employment Equality (Religion or Belief) Regulations 2003 (No. 1660).
3.   Taylor Stephen, Emir Astra. *Employment Law*. Oxford 2006; Chapter 9, pp 177-191.
4.   *Smith v Safeway plc* (1996) ICR 868.
5.   *Schmidt v Austicks Bookshops* (1977) ICR 85.
6.   'Woman loses fight to wear cross' at website: http://news.bbc. co.uk/1/hi/england/london/6165368.stm.

— 22 —

Medical fees

One of the privileges of being a doctor is the entitlement to medical fees for professional consultation and treatment. The basis of this entitlement stems from section 16 of the Medical Registration Ordinance, Chapter 161 of the Laws of Hong Kong. Subsection (1) confers the entitlement to a doctor to practise upon registration and to 'recover **reasonable charges** for professional aid, advice and visits and the value of any medicine or any medical or surgical appliances rendered, made or supplied to his patients'.

The reader may not at this point realise the privilege and might think that a non-registered doctor or bone-setter can equally charge his patients. It is indeed true that anyone registered or not can charge, but subsection (2) makes a difference. Subsection (2) stipulates that 'no person shall be entitled to recover in any court any such charges as are referred to in subsection (1) unless at the date when such charges accrued he was a registered medical practitioner'.

The difference should now be clear.

Another interesting issue is how much to charge. Apart from the word 'reasonable' in section 16(1) as quoted above, there seems nowhere in the law where further regulation of the amount of fees charged is mentioned. The medical practitioner therefore has a free hand to charge as he wishes so long as it is within reasonable limits.

The guideline is thus related to the **amount of fees** usually charged for similar treatments by other practitioners in the territory, and the experience and reputation of the clinician concerned. In addition, Paragraph 12.3 of Part II of the newly released Code of Professional

Conduct of the Medical Council of Hong Kong prohibits the charge of excessive fees and itemises the factors considered.

Still, so long as patients are willing to pay, it would seem that the exact magnitude of a charge is in real life extremely variable. It would seem that market forces are the main determinant of the charges which a particular doctor can make.

It is worth mentioning that various interested bodies but most notably the Hong Kong Medical Association have on several occasions since the late 90s surveyed the private sector of Hong Kong. There have been remarks in published reports from authorities that the Hong Kong laissez-faire health-care system does not really obey the free demand and supply model. The Hospital Authority is willingly or unwillingly basically a provider of ultimate last resort health care. Many people go to private doctors whenever they can afford it and then return to the public hospitals when their pockets are dry. Private doctors are thus free to charge as they like; the consequence is simply that patients' pockets can dry up earlier. There have been calls for **pricing regulation** of health care in order to prevent the monetary drain resulting from any possible further increase in health-care expenditure. This analysis may no longer be entirely true in the face of the changing economy and the changing pattern of future health-care financing. The author leaves the issue for readers' further thought.

References and Further Reading
1. Code of Professional Conduct of the Medical Council of Hong Kong.
2. Section 16 of the Medical Registration Ordinance, Chapter 161 of the Laws of Hong Kong.

— 23 —

Rebate

When the author was a young junior doctor, more than 20 plus years back, he was once told by a senior colleague who had just left the public hospital system for private practice that a lot of specialist doctors actually paid kickbacks in order to get referrals from primary care doctors. Likewise, doctors got kickbacks from laboratories for referrals for investigations. This information was purely hearsay and the author confesses that he has no real idea of the veracity of the allegations. It is simply an honest report of factual statements heard and there is no attempt to defame anyone or the profession.

Perhaps it may be said that the comment is not entirely without basis. There is bound to be someone brave enough to bend the rules.

Is the use of **kickbacks** alright?

Let us look at section 9 subsection 1 of the Prevention of Bribery Ordinance:

(1) Any agent who, without lawful authority or reasonable excuse, solicits or accepts any advantage as an inducement to or reward for or otherwise on account of his

    (a) doing or forbearing to do any act in relation to his principal's affairs or business; or

    (b) showing or forbearing to show favour or disfavour to any person in relation to his principal's affairs or business,

shall be guilty of an offence.

How does the statute apply to our situation? Here, the patient would be the **principal**, the referring doctor the **agent** and the laboratory the other party. Therefore, kickbacks would fall squarely within the meaning of the statute and can constitute **bribery** in law.

Apart from the law, section 14 of the Code of Professional Conduct on 'Improper financial transactions' also prohibits offering or acceptance of financial or other inducement for referrals.

The seriousness of the conduct is therefore clear.

Now that Hong Kong has become one of the 'cleanest' cities in the world in terms of corruption, we should not allow 'unfair competition' as such anymore in the profession.

References and Further Reading

1. Section 14 of the Code of Professional Conduct of the Medical Council of Hong Kong.
2. *Integrity in Practice: A Practical Guide for Medical Practitioners on Corruption Prevention*. ICAC and HKMA.

24

Restraining patients

Unlawful restraint is **battery** and perhaps also **false imprisonment**.

Patients, however, are not uncommonly restrained in the wards. Obviously, neither the hospital staff nor the medical practitioner enjoys any special powers in the law to restrain others. What then is the authority of the hospital staff to restrain people? How are we to protect ourselves? If we have no clear authority to do so, should we stop restraining patients?

These questions are indeed quite legitimate but we have a defence, and that is '**necessity**'. 'Necessity' in law means that damage is inflicted in order to avert more serious damage. Justification for the damage caused thus lies in the prevention of the latter. Therefore, to keep within the law and be protected by the defence of 'necessity', one has to be very cautious in executing restraint of patients.

What then are the elements of a **lawful restraint**? Restraint or physical control by mechanical limitation of movements of the patient must be aimed at reducing the risk of inadvertent injury to the patient's body. It should only be used when there is no alternative means of control such as sedation, counselling, or more constant supervision. The least amount of restraint for the minimal time period necessary for its purpose is to be employed. Regular reviews, clear documentation, and adequate explanation to the patient and relatives are also mandatory. Thus, the justification would be valid if restraint is imposed for preventing injury and it would not be sound if the purpose is, say, to lessen the burden of busy nursing staff.

If done within the restrictions described above, the necessity test is satisfied and since this is also within the remit of good medical practice as prescribed by authoritative organisations and institutional guidelines, the court will not disagree with the hospital staff over the practice.

There is no fear therefore if, but only if, one is vigilant in following the above details in ordering the restraint of a patient.

References and Further Reading

1. *Guide to Good Nursing Practice: Physical Restraint.* Nursing Council of Hong Kong 2008, available at website: http://www. nchk.org.hk/practice/physical_restraint_e.pdf.

25

Discharge against medical advice

There was once a 'working practice' in the public hospitals that patients who wished to leave hospital without the doctor's agreement were to sign a **Discharge against Medical Advice** (DAMA) form. The rule was so strongly ingrained that patients were 'warned' that a signature was a must and they would not be allowed to go without one. The author has witnessed nurses threatening to inform the police should patients be disinclined to follow the order. Indeed, the signing of the DAMA form was regarded as the more important 'pass' to be obtained before patients would be allowed to leave hospital compared with paying the hospital bill!

The reason for this practice is obscure. It could be that the nurses were so concerned for the welfare of the patients that they wanted to seek every means to keep them on the wards. It could also be that they would be required to write statements explaining why a patient should have gone without the doctor's discharge.

Strictly speaking, the patient has no obligation to sign anything or follow any instructions in order to leave a hospital against advice. The hospital has no right to keep anyone against his wishes. Neither does any person give up his right to free movement on admission into a hospital. Keeping a person from leaving therefore amounts in reality to unlawful detention, i.e. **false imprisonment**, and is no different from any ordinary person locking up another against the latter's will, in the absence of authority to do so.

What then could be the significance of signing such a form, if any? The point is that the signed form could well be taken as written **documentation** evidencing the fact that the doctors and nurses have discharged their duty of explaining to the patient the risk he is taking on his own in leaving. In this sense, it actually matters little if the patient refuses to sign as long as the staff have explained all that is required and recorded that clearly in the hospital notes, and timed, dated and signed them themselves.

The conclusion is that it falls on the patient's **good will** to cooperate and sign. If patients do not wish to, they still have every right to leave and, if members of staff have explained the risk, they should say so in the notes.

Having said that, it remains for the author to make the important qualification that there are always exceptions to any rule or doctrine.

Three common scenarios can be cited in relation to the context of DAMA and they concern: mental patients, certain contagious diseases and public safety considerations.

Any colleague who has been practising for a little while will be aware of Forms I, II and III, which are needed for patients suffering from a mental disorder of a nature or degree which warrants their detention in a mental hospital for observation or treatment, or to be so detained in the interests of their own health or safety or the protection of other persons, to be transferred for detention to a mental hospital. The legal basis conferring this power upon the medical practitioner is found in sections 31 and 32 of the Mental Health Ordinance (Chapter 136 of the Laws of Hong Kong).

The same principle would apply in the case of a patient who does not have sufficient mental capacity for other reasons, such as being under the influence of alcohol or drugs, for public safety reasons, as well as for the safety of the individual. In the case of minors, it is better if a minor waits for the arrival of a parent or guardian before being allowed to leave the hospital. There is no exact stipulation in the statutory law in this instance and much will depend upon the judgments of the hospital staff as to the mental maturity and safety of the minor if he or she was allowed to go without an accompanying parent or guardian.

A ready example of contagious diseases and public safety considerations restricting a patient's right of freedom to go was seen during the SARS pandemic, when persons suspected of having the disease and certain patients and contacts were kept in hospitals or isolation facilities for quarantine or treatment. The legal basis for such power is included under sections 22 (quarantine) and 23 (isolation) of the Prevention and Control of Disease Regulation (Chapter 599A of the Laws of Hong Kong). It is useful to remember that only three conditions fall under the heading of 'specified diseases' for the purpose of section 23 which is found in section 56 and they are SARS, swine flu and multi-resistant tuberculosis.

Obviously, a patient in a custodial ward is legally either serving a detention or under arrest pending prosecution. Such a person is not entitled to leave for home although he or she retains the right to refuse treatment and to go back to the police station or prison.

References and Further Reading
1. The Mental Health Ordinance (Chapter 136 of the Laws of Hong Kong), sections 31 and 32.
2. Prevention and Control of Disease Regulation (Chapter 599A of the Laws of Hong Kong), sections 22, 23 and 56.

— 26 —

Sick leave

The sick leave issue poses special difficulties for the doctor. It is often said that doctors are medically the least well-treated species on Earth. Very often we tend to be 'brave' and disregard 'minor' symptoms and ailments, telling ourselves they are no big deal. Doctors can also find it embarrassing and somewhat of a disgrace to be seen to be ill since they are viewed as healers and enemies of disease.

Young doctors, in particular, have a tendency to continue to go to work despite sickness. There is understandably pressure from busy schedules, from superiors and from self-image.

This behaviour, however, can be dangerous.

First, there is the risk of the **spreading of infectious diseases** like the common cold and influenza. We usually view such illnesses as minor and unimportant, but when a colleague is suffering from one we should really instead wish that he or she gets well soon.

Second, and the more important, is the risk of **committing mistakes** when one is unwell. It is not difficult to realise that the daily work of a doctor is full of multiple traps and snares, and if one is not on the alert with a clear head inadvertent errors are easily made. There is no concession for being heroic and continuing to work when ill. The standard of care and the duty to patients does not change for reasons of gallantry. Indeed, the straightforward answer to such an excuse would be that the doctor who is ill should not have come to work in the first place.

The conclusion that can be drawn is therefore that an ill doctor is a danger to others as well as to himself. It would be a better world if all supervisors could be more humane and understanding. A doctor who is ill has to judge whether he is fit enough to go to work and to bear the risks.

27

Absence of leave

Leave, or, more specifically annual leave, is something of an **entitlement** to an employee under suitable circumstances. Under section 41AA(1) of the Employment Ordinance, Chapter 57 of the Laws of Hong Kong, 'every employee who has been in employment under a continuous contract for not less than 12 months shall, in respect of each leave year, be entitled to paid leave'.

Doctors under employment should therefore refer to their **employment contract** to determine the specific details of their entitled rights.

An employer is under a duty to ensure that arrangements are made so that employees can take leave as agreed.

Payment in lieu of annual leave is dealt with in section 41E(1), which restricts such remuneration subject essentially to subsection 2:

'(2)   Where an employee is entitled to more than 10 days' annual leave in respect of a particular leave year, he may, in lieu of taking part of the leave, work on not more than the number of days by which such annual leave exceeds 10, and in case an employee so agrees, the amount payable to him in respect of any such day shall not be less than the aggregate of

   (a)   the wages receivable by him in respect of the period worked; and

   (b)   the annual leave pay he would have received had he been granted leave.'

Put more simply, an employee must at least take 10 continuous days of annual leave in a year and he is entitled to additional payment for the other days of entitled leave worked.

Another issue of common concern is **sick leave**. Entitlement to sickness allowance is found under section 33. This only applies to an employee under a continuous contract for a period of 1 month or more immediately preceding a sickness day. The rate is 2 days of paid sickness leave for each completed month during the first 12 months of employment, and 4 days for each month thereafter. It is possible to accumulate up to a maximum of 120 paid sickness days.

Subject to certain exceptions, an employee has to take more than 4 consecutive days of sickness leave to be entitled to be paid sickness allowance. It is for this reason that patients often ask for 4 or more days of sick leave, which obviously provides no excuse for the medical practitioner to let loose his discretion.

Lastly, an employer who terminates a contract of employment on any sickness day in respect of which sickness allowance is payable commits an offence and is also liable to pay compensation to the employee.

References and Further Reading
1.   Employment Ordinance, Chapter 57 of the Laws of Hong Kong.

28

Off-duty working

The author once overheard the head of a clinical department boasting how devoted and committed his staff was. He claimed that his staff would all volunteer to work 7 days a week despite the introduction of the 5-day week. Another story relating to off-duty work was that of a hospital executive instructing one of her senior staff members who had accumulated surplus leave to take leave on alternate days and to take work home on those leave days!

Whether these represent good management strategies or mean staff handling is entirely personal opinion. What is more interesting perhaps is the **legal implication** of working during off-duty hours.

The critical issue will be whether staff members are really working **voluntarily** during the off-duty hours, or whether they do so from **submission** under duress. Using one's position of power or authority to exercise undue influence on staff to work in contravention of the rules set out in the Employment Ordinance is clearly illegal.

The other problem is that of liability should any arise in the course of such 'work'. Is it work? Does the liability arise '**in the course of employment**'? Is the employer vicariously liable? Is the person who exerts the pressure to 'coerce' people to come to work 'voluntarily' given the authority to represent the institution to take such measures to the extent that the institution should be held liable? Would that superior be personally held responsible in the absence of such authority? What about insurance coverage? These are the questions which need to be resolved before making a 'light' decision.

A better approach is perhaps to encourage staff to make good use of their holidays so as to be recharged for future work, as many really enlightened supervisors recommend.

References and Further Reading
1.   Employment Ordinance, Chapter 57 of the Laws of Hong Kong.

29

The diagnosis on sick leave certificates

An attending doctor of course has a duty to issue a sick leave certificate when requested by a patient who is unfit to work. As in so many of the given privileges to the members of the profession, a high standard of ethics is presumed. We are, however, not talking about the obvious here. Thus, it needs no reminder that issuance for monetary return without a genuine belief of unfitness to work is dishonest conduct.

The issue the author wants to raise here is whether the doctor should put down the exact medical diagnosis on the sick leave certificate. The current practice is that only some doctors do. Those who do not will instead just write something like 'surgical illness'. Which is preferred?

To determine the most appropriate course of action, one should not forget that the duty is merely to issue a certificate to prove **unfitness to work** and nothing more. There is no obligation to inform the employer of the nature of the patient's illness. Indeed, it may be dangerous to do so for fear of breaching the duty of confidentiality owed by a doctor to his or her patient. One may argue that if the patient expressly asks for the illness to be described, the doctor should do so. Yes, that could be taken as **verbal consent** to disclose one's private matters to a third party, but it is really only verbal. What if the patient denies any such request 2 months later? Perhaps by then neither the doctor nor the patient will recall exactly what was said. Ask the patient to sign a written consent and file that in the records!

The author never writes a diagnosis even when urged to by patients because that is simply outside the scope of a doctor's duty in issuing a sick leave certificate. Quite simply, many a time patients actually want a specific diagnosis on the certificate in order to claim insurance compensation. This would be an **ulterior motive** to satisfy an incidental and collateral purpose not originally intended to be within the ambit of the certificate. The proper channel to get a diagnosis and/or any details of the medical treatment would be a medical report, which every patient is entitled to request. The reader will recall that in requesting the hospital for a medical report, the patient is required to sign an application form which would then serve as evidence of his request.

30

Sick leave or attendance certificate?

These days it is customary for doctors to print standard documents from their desk-top computers in relation to their work. One of these many standard documents often requested by patients is the sick leave certificate. Some patients, though, specifically ask for attendance certificates instead. What actually is the difference between these two documents?

A '**sick leave**' **certificate** is evidence issued by a registered medical practitioner conferring entitlement to be absent from work by reason of a person being unfit to work on account of injury or sickness. An '**attendance**' **certificate**, on the other hand, is a certification of the patient having attended the issuing doctor's clinic for consultation or treatment.

The resulting effect of these two documents for the purpose of obtaining sick leave is probably the same. However, all depends in reality on the exact wordings of the terms of the contract of employment. This is even more so when one is talking about **sickness compensation**. Often people also would be looking for insurance claims and then the terms of the **insurance** contract would be relevant. Normally neither the patient nor the doctor would know about these terms or have the time to find out, and in this sense a sick leave certificate would be more likely to offer a better cover.

On some occasions patients do ask for attendance certificates only and it may be the case here that they want to preserve their 'clean record'. Others may just be too busy and plan to go back to work for the rest of the day and do not need a full day off.

——— 31 ———

Medical reports

Newly qualified doctors on completion of their internship and registration will in no time find themselves involved in writing medical reports. This is more often likely if they work in specialties treating acute injuries and accidents, although practically no one engaged in clinical practice is immune.

Medical reports can be for a variety of purposes. They can be for the patient's continuation of treatment upon referral or after emigration. They may be for claiming compensation from insurance companies. They may also be for the purposes of court proceedings.

In the old days, when medical facts such as the nature of an injury were required to be provided by the attending doctor, there was no alternative but to have the doctor in court to answer what the court wanted to know. This was seen as taking away precious time attending patients as it often was (and still is) the case that one might have to wait in turn for some while for the case to be heard. The rule now in force is that doctors' factual evidence is equally accepted and admissible in **written form**. Only when further clarification or additional facts are wanted would a medical practitioner be required to attend in person. This move clearly is welcomed from the point of view of the busy medical practitioner and could be considered a privilege the court has provided for the medical profession.

The legal requirements for the medical report for this purpose are found in subsection (2) of section 65B of the Criminal Procedure Ordinance, Chapter 221 of the Laws of Hong Kong. The statement has to be signed by the doctor who wrote it and he must declare that the statement is 'true to the best of his knowledge and belief'. The latter explains why the secretaries always add that 'remark' in your script when they do the typing. Under subsections 4(a) and (b), both the opposite party and the court may require attendance of the person making the statement to give evidence.

Doctors who end up attending courts are often left wondering whether they are entitled to the **fees** for witnesses. The older generation of Government doctors invariably told their juniors that they weren't and that was correct. These days most public doctors are employees of the Hospital Authority and are no longer civil servants and so the story is different. Strictly, if the doctor is attending on behalf of the Authority, i.e. in the course of his employment when attending court, he should not be earning extra money unless there is an express stipulation of such entitlement. The money should in theory go to the Hospital Authority. A doctor attending court in his own capacity, as in the case of a doctor in his own private practice, on the other hand, should be fully entitled.

References and Further Reading

1. Section 65B of the Criminal Procedure Ordinance, Chapter 221 of the Laws of Hong Kong.
2. Patrick Chan (editor-in-chief). *Hong Kong Civil Procedure* (The White Book) 2009 Volume 1 Order 62 Costs Second Schedule 62/App/52 - 62/App/55. Sweet & Maxwell.

32

Sexual harassment

Sexual harassment may potentially occur in any employment context and knowledge of the issue should be of relevance to the medical practitioner as much as it is to any ordinary citizen. It has been defined by the courts as '**unwanted conduct** of a personal nature or other conduct based on sex affecting the dignity of **women and men** at work' (*British Telecommunications v Williams* [1997]).

A form of direct discrimination, sexual harassment can range from sex-based comments which make the recipient feel degraded to serious sexual assault.

Classic cases where the motivation is sexual fit easily into the Sex Discrimination Ordinance. It is, however, often overlooked that it is the subjective effect on the harassed that counts, not the objective offensiveness. An identical joke, for example, may be sexual harassment in one case and not so in another. Motive and intention are irrelevant. Also, harassment does not have to be by a man against a woman. It can equally be by a woman against a man, or by a man against another man, so long as a woman would not have been treated in the same way.

To prove **direct discrimination**, one has to be treated less favourably than the opposite sex and to suffer a detriment therefrom.

Two issues are equally relevant to the medical practitioner: to avoid one's conduct falling within the definition of sexual harassment, and to be able to identify when one is subject to sexual harassment.

Where the degrading conduct is committed by another employee, the employer is potentially vicariously liable for any discrimination. In addition, the failure of an employer to investigate a reported allegation may also amount to a further act of discrimination, if, but for the complainant's sex, it would have been investigated. An employer may wish to adopt a **company policy** and make sure that any complaint is properly investigated and acted upon. If confirmed, action should be against the perpetrator, not the victim.

The promotion of **public knowledge** about sexual harassment and its elimination are among the many important functions of the Equal Opportunities Commission (EOC).

A claim for sexual harassment can be brought directly to the District Court. It can also go through the EOC, whereby, after initial assessment, a recommendation will be made to the EOC Legal and Complaints Committee, which decides whether to grant assistance. Factors considered include whether the case raises a question of principle and whether the case is so complex that it is unreasonable to expect unaided litigation. Assistance may include giving legal advice and legal representation.

References and Further Reading

1. *British Telecommunications v Williams* (1997) IRLR 668.
2. Sex Discrimination Ordinance, Chapter 480 of the Laws of Hong Kong.
3. The website of the Equal Opportunities Commission of Hong Kong at http://www.eoc.org.hk/eoc/GraphicsFolder/default.aspx.

33

Am I being harassed?

Harassment is a word in vogue and we hear it being used all the time. To give a good universal definition is, however, not so easy because it is used frequently in daily spoken English to mean different things and its law meaning also differs according to the jurisdiction under consideration. Generally **harassment** refers to a wide range of offensive behaviour which alarms, distresses, upsets, threatens, or disturbs.

It is the **conduct** that offends and this can be non-verbal, verbal, or physical, or combinations of these. Whether the conduct offends will in turn depend on the **subjective** interpretation of the harassed.

In Hong Kong, there is no specific legislation against harassment per se like the Protection from Harassment Act 1997 of the United Kingdom. Although this latter piece of legislation is not directly enforceable in Hong Kong, therefore, it is helpful to look at the offence since it assists in an understanding of the subject. Section 4 of the English Protection from Harassment Act 1997 states:

4   Putting people **in fear** of violence

(1)   A person whose course of conduct causes another to fear, on at least two occasions, that violence will be used against him, is guilty of an offence if he knows or ought to know that his course of conduct will cause the other so to fear on each of those occasions.

(2)   For the purposes of this section, the person whose course of conduct is in question ought to know that it will cause another to fear that violence will be used against him on any occasion if a reasonable person in possession of the same information would think the

course of conduct would cause the other so to fear on that occasion.

The only references to harassment we have in the legislation of Hong Kong are found in three statutes which are in relation to particular contexts. They are:

A.   Sex Discrimination Ordinance – Section 2

(5)   For the purposes of this Ordinance, a person (howsoever described) **sexually harasses** a woman if

(a)   the person

(i)   makes an unwelcome sexual advance, or an unwelcome request for sexual favours, to her; or

(ii)   engages in other unwelcome conduct of a sexual nature in relation to her, in circumstances in which a reasonable person, having regard to all the circumstances, would have anticipated that she would be offended, humiliated or intimidated; or

(b)   the person, alone or together with other persons, engages in conduct of a sexual nature which creates a hostile or intimidating environment for her.

B.   **Disability** Discrimination Ordinance – Section 2

(6)   For the purposes of this Ordinance, a person (howsoever described) harasses another person if that first-mentioned person engages in unwelcome conduct (which may include an oral or written statement) on account of that second-mentioned person's disability, or on account of the disability of an associate of that second-mentioned person, in circumstances in which a reasonable person, having regard to all the circumstances, would have anticipated that the second-mentioned person would be offended, humiliated or intimidated by that conduct.

C. Race Discrimination Ordinance – Section 7
   Racial harassment
   (1) In any circumstances relevant for the purposes of any provision of this Ordinance, a person harasses another person if, on the grounds of the race of that other person or a near relative of that other person, the first-mentioned person engages in unwelcome conduct (which may include an oral or a written statement), in circumstances in which a reasonable person, having regard to all the circumstances, would have anticipated that the other person would be offended, humiliated or intimidated by that conduct.
   (2) In any circumstances relevant for the purposes of any provision of this Ordinance, a person ('the first-mentioned person') harasses another person ('the second-mentioned person') if, on the grounds of the race of the second-mentioned person or his or her near relative, the first-mentioned person, alone or together with other persons, engages in conduct (which may include an oral or a written statement) that creates a hostile or intimidating environment for the second-mentioned person.

To illustrate how we can apply the above in action in pursuing a remedy, let us examine the case of *Yuen Sha Sha v Tse Chi Pan* DCEO 1/1998, where the plaintiff was supported by the Equal Opportunities Commission of Hong Kong. The plaintiff was a third-year female student at the Chinese University of Hong Kong. The defendant, a male student residing in the same hall, surreptitiously took videos of her of a personal nature inside her room and shared them with a friend. The plaintiff successfully claimed damages and costs pursuant to section 76(6), 76(3A)(e) and (f) of the Sex Discrimination Ordinance.

It is hoped that the above provides the reader with a better knowledge of the concept of harassment and better able to assess his/ her own position.

References and Further Reading

1. Section 4 of the English Protection from Harassment Act 1997.
2. Sex Discrimination Ordinance, Section 2.
3. Disability Discrimination Ordinance, Section 2.
4. Race Discrimination Ordinance, Section 7.
5. *Yuen Sha Sha v Tse Chi Pan* DCEO 1/1998.

34

Intimacy with patients or their relatives!

Let us begin with a true story. A young, attractive air hostess was seen in the plastic surgery out-patients for a follow-up. She had sustained a fracture to the mandible from a fall after fainting at 3am on the way home following a drink with friends. The fracture was well fixed but she had to abstain from eating hard food for 6 weeks to allow time for the fracture to heal properly.

At the follow-up consultation she asked the doctor whether he could go out to dinner with her to 'teach' her what to eat. She then moved her chair closer and grasped the doctor's hand. The doctor took her hand in his other hand and gently replaced it on the desk. The patient then asked the doctor if he would examine her heart, suggesting that she might have also injured her chest during the fall. She went on to unbutton her shirt, which was of a tight fit and clearly revealed her figure.

The doctor immediately asked her to wait until he could get a nurse along as chaperone. Nurses were in short supply and they were shared between consultation rooms, which all opened at the rear into a long wide corridor. While waiting for the nurse, the doctor checked his computer and retrieved a chest X-ray taken at the time of admission; this showed no abnormalities apart from shadows of nipple rings. Meanwhile the young lady was loosening her brassiere.

What would you do next?

This is an extreme example but a real one experienced by the author. In daily medical practice, there are certainly a lot of situations which could potentially allow for the development of **emotional attachment** more than called for normally in the doctor's encounter with patients or their relatives. It is the case that a psychiatrist may intimately explore a patient's mind; a dermatologist might have a real need to ask for a sexual history; a surgeon may be allowed the right to touch the breasts; the gynaecologist may need to examine the private parts of the body; the conscientious doctor may have to see the patient's daughter repeatedly to inform her of progress and share decision-making, etc. Each and every encounter can plant the seeds of an emotional attachment as a result of the trust and confidence inherent in the doctor-patient relationship.

The more open-minded may argue why it is not possible for true love to exist simply because the person is or was your patient or the latter's relative. Nevertheless, it is also easy to realise that there may be an element of immorality if a doctor allows an **intimate relationship** to arise out of the clinical context. Furthermore, such conduct is unethical and is also conceivable as a breach of fiduciary duty.

Variously labelled as '**sexual misconduct**', '**sexual impropriety**', or '**professional incest**', the concern this time for such behaviour is not so much a breach of the law or whether you are protected because you have valid consent for the intimacy. What is relevant is breach of professional ethics and abuse of trust and confidence. The new Code of Professional Conduct classifies such a relationship as professional misconduct and the Council would take a serious view towards this, Section G of Part II, Paragraph 25 subparagraph 1. It is something which should be avoided at all costs and must be ceased if it begins to develop.

'Once a patient, always a patient': there is no former patient in this regard. Some jurisdictions prescribe a **safety period** of 2 years, i.e. unsafe period, after which a green light is given to relationships. Authorities, though, have pointed out the difficulties in proving the termination of a professional link if there has been contact between the parties. The better view is therefore a permanent 'flashing red light' and a definite stop sign once a doctor-patient relationship is established.

An article entitled 'Drawing the line' in the May 2008 issue of Casebook published by the Medical Protection Society deliberated on the issue. The **warning signs** listed in this article warrant recapitulation because the situation is one which is best avoided. They are: frequently thinking about the patient personally; longing to see her with anticipation; allowing a consultation to run on without medical cause; giving preferential treatment without a good reason; special concessions like divulging personal information; and creating opportunities to see the patient.

An illustrative account is found in the recent judgment of the Medical Council inquiry MC 2929/4/E and MC 1/2929/4/E dated 1 May 2009. In this highly educational case, a public hospital psychiatrist was found guilty of, among other things, having an improper sexual relationship with one of his patients for a period of 9 years. In view of the gravity of the offence, the defendant doctor was removed from the register for the first time ever merely upon publication of the order in the Gazette so as to prevent any delay by further legal procedures of appeal. The rationale being that the defendant was considered to pose a danger to the public.

The message is to be professional, know your boundaries, and **take control**. 'Professionalism must be maintained and must also be seen to be maintained.'

'And lead us not into temptation, but deliver us from evil… ' Matthew 6.13.

References and Further Reading
1. Sandy Anthony, Sara Williams. *Drawing the line*. Medical Protection Society 2008; 16(2): 8-10.
2. Code of Professional Conduct of the Medical Council of Hong Kong, Section G of Part II, Paragraph 25 subparagraph 1.
3. Medical Council inquiry judgment MC 2929/4/E and MC 1/2929/4/E, 2009 available on the web at http://www.mchk.org.hk/docs/STW_20090501.pdf.
4. *Professional Boundaries: A Nurse's Guide to the Importance of Appropriate Professional Boundaries.* National Council of the State Boards of Nursing, USA 2007 available on the web at https://www.ncsbn.org/Professional_Boundaries_2007_Web.pdf.
5. The Bible: the Gospel according to St. Matthew 6.13.

35

Dishonesty

Doctors are intelligent people. There is no doubting that. The author still recalls the previous dean of the medical school of the University of Hong Kong on the occasion of an annual prize giving day ceremony. In his introductory speech he said, 'Every year the top 2 per cent of the cohort of secondary school students enters the university. The top 2 per cent of that lot enters the medical faculty. The top 2 per cent of those who enter the medical faculty each year end up here tonight. I must call you the cream of the ivory tower.' The author happened on that occasion to be a prize winner.

Honesty is a basic **human virtue**. It is also an essential feature of an **ethical professional practice**. Is it possible to hide one's dishonesty by using intelligence? How does the court overcome an intelligent dishonest person? A story will tell.

In *R v Ghosh* (1984), a locum consultant surgeon in the National Health Service fraudulently claimed that he had carried out an operation and that money was due to him. He maintained that he had not acted dishonestly because he did not regard such conduct as dishonest. This is obviously a wise answer because dishonesty refers to the state of mind of the accused not the conduct itself.

Such wisdom was, however, to no avail in the eyes of the law. The court 'proclaimed' the test for dishonesty as consisting of two components:

- The objective test – Would an honest and reasonable person regard the behaviour in question as dishonest? If not, the accused is not dishonest. If yes, the subjective test is applied to the accused.

- The subjective test – Did the accused realise that an honest and reasonable person would regard such behaviour as dishonest? If yes, he is dishonest. If no, he may be acquitted.

It is therefore the subjective knowledge that others would regard the behaviour as dishonest that matters, not the subjective view of the accused of the behaviour.

The surgeon's appeal against his own conviction in the English Court of Appeal was thus dismissed.

References and Further Reading

1. *R v Ghosh* (1984) QB 1053.
2. Smith John. *Smith & Hogan Criminal Law*, 9th edn. Butterworths 1999; Chapter 16, pp 536-540.

36

Inadvertent dishonesty

As mentioned in the previous chapter, honesty is a basic human virtue. No one would dispute that.

Even a cunning person should have no reason to act in a dishonest manner unless it is for a 'good' purpose.

No one should therefore choose to be dishonest.

Doctors are professionals highly regarded in the eyes of the public. Any dishonesty found in a doctor's practice is inexcusable.

How does the profession itself look at dishonesty? The answer can be found in the Code of Professional Conduct under Misconduct in a Professional Respect. Dishonesty is regarded as misconduct.

Obviously, dishonesty is highly damaging as far as the reputation of a person is concerned. It can also potentially have immense bearings on one's career.

The issue then is who would dare to be dishonest? The tricky point here is that it is possible to be '**inadvertently**' **dishonest** if one is not careful.

An example will illustrate the point. The author once heard of a case where a house officer topped up a sample of blood meant for the purpose of cross-matching for an elective operation. Her reason for so doing was that she had failed to take the required amount. The short-fall was discovered by the laboratory. The house officer remarked that she was innocent because she had learnt to do this from her predecessors.

Is she really innocent?

This is how the author would analyse the matter:

1. The doctor concerned had full knowledge of the required volume of blood as evinced by her conduct in topping-up.

2. She was attempting to represent to the laboratory that the right volume had been obtained when she sent the specimen.

3. This was an intentional act as she had chosen to do it voluntarily on her own initiative.

4. She was therefore trying to deceive the laboratory.

5. Such an act would be dishonest to a right-minded person.

6. It also cannot be denied that she should know that the act was dishonest in the eyes of a right-minded person in view of her educational background.

7. It is therefore submitted that she was dishonest both objectively and subjectively in committing the said act.

8. Being taught by predecessors how to cut corners is no defence because a mature, responsible, prudent, highly educated medical graduate is expected to be able, and has a duty, to exercise reasonable care in making judgments and acting on them.

However unfortunate the case, the consequences for the young doctor here could have been devastating. Two lessons are to be learnt here: exercise **caution** and **think twice** before you believe and follow.

How does the court decide if one is dishonest? The test the courts use is that which originated from the case mentioned in the previous chapter of *R v Ghosh* (1982). A locum consultant surgeon in the National Health Service falsely claimed money for an operation which was actually done by a colleague not himself. In the trial, he wisely insisted that he did not regard that the conduct was dishonest and therefore he had not been dishonest. The way the court looked at the issue has now become the standard test for dishonesty in the courts. The court analysed the issue in a two-step manner:

1. Objectively – whether an honest reasonable person in the circumstances would regard the act as dishonest; and

2. Subjectively – whether the defendant should know that an honest reasonable person in the circumstances would regard the act as dishonest.

If both of these two elements are satisfied, the defendant would be regarded as dishonest. The fact that a defendant honestly or dishonestly thinks that the conduct is honest is thus irrelevant.

It is submitted that the unlucky young doctor found topping-up the blood must be dishonest applying the *Ghosh* test.

References and Further Reading

1. *R v Ghosh* (1984) QB 1053.
2. Smith John. *Smith & Hogan Criminal Law*, 9th edn. Butterworths 1999; Chapter 16, pp 536-540.

37

Abortion

This time the author wants to start with the question, 'Is the law rigid?' Some may say yes, some may say no. But please be reminded that 'rigid' is not the same as 'harsh'.

For those who answer 'yes', they have a point. That is that the law has to provide **certainty**. This is a very important criterion of a good legal system because people must be able to foretell what is and what is not an infringement and how serious any breach of the law is going to be.

On the other hand, the characteristic of a common law system, i.e. that to which the Hong Kong system belongs, is that it is at the same time flexible. **Flexibility** is catered for in the system in the deliberations made by the court in relation to the particular circumstances of a case, the weight given to mitigating factors and the degree of leniency in sentencing.

I want to illustrate this feature of flexibility with an interesting example drawn from the history of medicine.

The layman will say that abortion is nowadays legal. The well-informed medical practitioner will know that abortion is legal subject to certain provisos. This is clearly stated in statute. However, the situation was not so simple for our former colleagues not so very long ago.

This was the case when the trial of *R v Bourne* took place in 1939 when abortion was not yet legalised. A well-respected obstetrician 'of the highest skill' at St. Mary's Hospital in London, knowing that it was illegal but moved by compassion to help a 15-year-old girl who had been brutally raped and thereby made pregnant, performed an abortion 'without secrecy'.

He ended up being indicted and was tried for the criminal offence of unlawfully procuring a miscarriage, under section 58 of the Offences against the Person Act 1861.

The flexibility was evinced by the argument of the trial judge Lord MacNaghten (strictly, MacNaghten J, as he then was), in terms of what was regarded as the necessity of circumstances. In his summing up to the jury, he contended that both the mental and physical health of the girl would have suffered. Doubtlessly moved by the well-versed direction, the jury returned a verdict of not guilty, a most unusual eventuality indeed in those days.

It was not until 1967 that the Abortion Act came into effect in England. In Hong Kong, the abortion statutes are now found under sections 46 to 48 of the Offences against the Person Ordinance, Chapter 212 of the Laws of Hong Kong. Section 47A (medical termination of pregnancy) is where the exceptions are found which exempt the modern doctor from criminal liability when those conditions stipulated are fulfilled.

The above is also incidentally illustrative of how the law develops in line with the needs and social values of a society.

References and Further Reading

1. *R v Bourne* (1939) 1 KB 687.
2. Smith John. *Smith & Hogan Criminal Law*, 9th edn. Butterworths 1999; Chapter 12, pp 393-398.
3. Offences against the Person Ordinance, Chapter 212 of the Laws of Hong Kong.
4. Padfield N. *Criminal Law*, 2nd edn. Butterworths Core Text Series 2000; Chapter 5, pp 101-102.

___ 38 ___

Drink driving

No one these days should be unfamiliar with the term 'drink driving'. Incidentally, doctors often have the occasion to go out to meet friends and colleagues or to attend lectures and seminars which involve some degree of social drinking. At the same time, many doctors have to travel between hospitals and very often at a very early stage of their career they become addicted to driving themselves.

Two potential consequences can arise from drink driving for doctors.

The first is infringement of the **traffic offences**. In addition to section 38 'careless driving' and section 39 'dangerous driving', there are also the specific offences of 'driving, attempting to drive or being in charge of a motor vehicle under the influence of drink or drugs', section 39, and, the same 'with alcohol concentration above the prescribed limit', section 40, of the Road Traffic Ordinance, Chapter 374 of the Laws of Hong Kong. All of these are offences punishable by imprisonment.

The second is the possible consequence on registration and therefore the licence to practise medicine. It is recalled that under Part II of the Professional Code and Conduct issued by the Medical Council of Hong Kong, conviction of an **offence punishable with imprisonment** is reportable to the Council and there is a duty on the part of the concerned doctor to do so. Such an offence is also possible grounds for withdrawal of a doctor's licence. Paragraph 11 subparagraph 1 of the new Code of Professional Conduct now makes it more explicit: 'Convictions for offences arising from drunkenness or abuse of alcohol or drugs (such as driving under the influence of alcohol or drugs) are likely to be regarded as professional misconduct.' In Section H Paragraph 27 subparagraph 2, it is expressly stated that alcohol and drug-related offences may affect a doctor's fitness to practise and are of particular concern to the Council.

The consequences are therefore heavy and much more so when compared with the case of an ordinary person. It is better to use a taxi service, as is advertised, when one has been drinking.

It is also interesting to note in passing that the previous strategy of refusal or delaying the **breath test** may no longer work. Under sections 39B(6) and 39C(15) respectively, failing to provide a specimen of breath for breath test screening without reasonable excuse, or, failing to provide a specimen of breath for breath analysis or a specimen of blood or urine for laboratory test without reasonable excuse, are now also offences punishable with imprisonment.

Medical practitioners should also note the recent changes in the law against drink driving. From 9 February 2009, police officers in uniform can require a person driving or attempting to drive on the road to undergo a breath screening test even in the **absence of any reasonable suspicion** of that person having been drinking (section 39B(1)), as was formerly needed. The legal basis for this is the Road Traffic Legislation (Amendment) Ordinance 2008. Penalties for drink driving as a result of this recent Ordinance have also been increased.

The message is thus crystal clear: Don't drink and drive.

References and Further Reading
1. Road Traffic Ordinance, Chapter 374 of the Laws of Hong Kong.
2. Road Traffic Legislation (Amendment) Ordinance 2008.
3. Paragraph 11 subparagraph 1, Code of Professional Conduct of the Medical Council of Hong Kong.

39

Appearance in magazines

Doctors do appear in newspapers and magazines as everyone knows. This can be as a result of the doctor or his medical institution releasing some information of public importance, or, the press approaching the medical profession for information on what they want to report.

There are a number of tricky areas which a doctor intending to approach the public may need to take note of:

- Make very sure that what is reported is **what you said**
- Make very sure that what is reported is **not only part** of what you said
- Make very sure that what you said is **not altered** in meaning
- If feasible, request a list in advance of the questions to be answered
- Provide facts that are evidence-based **without exaggeration** or creating unrealistic expectations
- Give only opinions that are **true and honest**
- Make very sure that any picture taken is **used properly and appropriately**
- Make very sure that you and your titles and qualifications are quoted (or not quoted) properly
- Make sure that you or your opinions are not used in any political scandal or attack directly or indirectly
- Make sure that you are not being promoted as being associated with any particular **association** in your practice
- Make sure that you are not being used for **practice promotion** by others

- Make very sure that you have the **chance to check** and alter the final draft of a report if it is an article to be published
- Declare any **conflict of interest**
- Avoid any unjustified direct or indirect **undermining** of the competency or integrity of other medical practitioners.

The above list is easy enough to check but it could be difficult in practice to guarantee. Any risk or liability is entirely that of the doctor concerned. A serious and cautious attitude may be warranted. Advice from more senior and experienced colleagues is often worth taking.

References and Further Reading

1. *A Guide for Doctors on Handling the Media*. Medical Protection Society 2008.

40

Medical photography

Doctors are used to taking photographs of their clinical findings, e.g. interesting physical signs, operative procedures, pre- and postoperative pictures, etc. These pictures are taken for a variety of purposes such as record keeping, teaching, presentations, and for use in publications and books.

Strictly speaking it is a form of **data collection** in taking pictures where the identity of the person being photographed can be traced. Even if the face does not appear on the picture, if the photos are filed in a collection and under a system from which the identity of the individual can be traced and retrieved, it is already within the ambits of the Personal Data (Privacy) Ordinance, Chapter 486 of the Laws of Hong Kong.

Schedule 1 of that Ordinance requires data collection to be fair, lawful, not excessive and necessary. In particular, it expressly stipulates that the data subject must be fully informed of the purpose of the data collection. Presumably therefore it is up to that person to refuse the collection.

In law, the **copyright of a photo** belongs to the photographer, the creator of the work. This is because a photograph is a piece of artistic work under section 2 of the Copyright Ordinance, Chapter 528 of the Laws of Hong Kong.

Not uncommonly clinical photos do reveal private parts of the body or in any case, parts of the body not supposed to be seen in public. The medical practitioner keeping such a collection would then have to be very cautious in keeping the pictures out of the public domain. Potentially one who releases or leaks such information could have infringed the Personal Data (Privacy) Ordinance and also committed the tort of breach of confidence.

The author personally lost a large collection of his clinical photos when a hard disk suddenly without warning broke down. In view of the ease of the information being duplicated and abused if the machine was sent for repair, it was decided that it was better to collect new photos rather than to take any risk.

It can therefore be a heavy burden if you are a serious and cautious person, both in terms of keeping a collection of clinical photos as well as keeping it safe.

References and Further Reading

1. Personal Data (Privacy) Ordinance, Chapter 486 of the Laws of Hong Kong.
2. Section 2 of the Copyright Ordinance, Chapter 528 of the Laws of Hong Kong.

41

Videotaping gynaecological examinations

One day in the medical officers' office of his department, the author was 'disturbed' by a loud cry of surprise from a female colleague. She was reading a newspaper. A young male doctor, who had been a classmate of hers at medical school, had been charged by the police for secretly videotaping gynaecological examinations of patients, which he performed in his clinic, and keeping them on his computer.

The immediate issue which was raised was what legal grounds there were to incriminate such a person or conduct. In simple words, what was wrong?

What are the possible legal grounds for pursuing this sort of impropriety? Some potential lines of approach are:

– Personal Data (Privacy) Ordinance: data collection principle 1 that collection has to be lawful and fair would have been violated. **Covert collection of personal data** is generally considered unfair in the absence of overriding public interest. This approach would work only if there was a system for retrieving the identity of the victims;

– Tort of **breach of confidence**: if there is any sharing of the recorded videos to a third party;

– **Breach of** the **trust** and confidence in the doctor-patient relationship;

– **Sexual harassment** under section 40(1) of the Sex Discrimination Ordinance (Cap 480) for 'unwelcomed conduct of a sexual nature', with a little straining;

– **Breach of contract**: on the premises that there is an implied term that the activities of the doctor are limited to what is required of the examination and no more unless additional consent is obtained.

The reader will immediately see that none of the above is quite specific to the wrongdoing, even if they are viable. It may indeed be a surprise to the reader to know that at this moment there is no specific remedy for **invasion of privacy** per se in the English common law (and so in Hong Kong). The exceptions are where there is the possibility of a **collateral cause of action**, e.g. defamation, malicious falsehood, intentional infliction of emotional stress, copyright infringement, nuisance, trespass, or one or more of the above mentioned remedies. This is confirmed in the famous English case of *Kaye v Robertson* (1991), where the well-known actor Gordon Kaye was photographed in his hospital bed by the press suffering from serious injuries, despite clear notices forbidding this outside his room. The court held that there was no right of action for breach of a person's privacy and such does not of itself entitle one to relief. This lack of protection of a person's privacy is in contrast to the laws of some other western countries such as the United States, France and Germany. The Law Reform Commission of Hong Kong actually started looking into the issue of a possible statutory tort of intrusion of privacy in Hong Kong in the mid-90s, and published its recommendation in a report in December 2004. So far we are still awaiting further action from the legislature.

The lacuna in the law is somewhat astonishing if one recalls what is in the Basic Law of the HKSAR, the International Covenant on Civil and Political Rights and the Hong Kong Bill of Rights, which are principles directly affecting the territory.

The reader may wonder in passing what charges are usually brought against the 'fashionable' mischief of taking 'beneath-the-skirt' pictures of ladies' underwear using cellular phones. For want of a better offence, it used to be 'loitering with intent' and more recently is 'behaving in a disorderly manner in a public place' (section 17B(2) of the Public Order Ordinance, Chapter 245 of the Laws of Hong Kong). Again one wonders why such an unwanted and common offence does not merit a more specific charge.

References and Further Reading

1. *Kaye v Robertson* (1991) FSR 62.
2. Section 39(3), Sex Discrimination Ordinance, Chapter 480 of the Laws of Hong Kong.
3. Basic Law of the HKSAR.
4. International Covenant on Civil and Political Rights.
5. Hong Kong Bill of Rights.
6. Section 17B(2), Public Order Ordinance, Chapter 245 of the Laws of Hong Kong.

42

Surveillance at work

A young professor in the hospital in which the author worked once came up with an interesting innovation. The laboratory assistant was for some reason refusing to process specimens at the expected speed and claimed to be very busy all the time. The professor 'wisely' attached to his desktop computer a surveillance camera, which he placed in the laboratory to monitor her. The laboratory assistant was extremely annoyed and threatened to sue him, although no action was ever actually taken. She was dismissed subsequently.

It is not difficult to see the conflict between an employer's monitoring, on the one hand, and the employee's privacy, on the other. Employers would argue that there is no such thing as employee's privacy at work, for their time is paid for. **Pervasive surveillance**, on the other hand, can be related to stress at work and psychological damage.

The interesting point here is whether there is really a case in law. Can we legitimately watch over our employees or staff with a camera? Can they sue us for so doing?

The answer to this seemingly straightforward issue is actually not a simple one.

Covert surveillance has been a hot topic in town in the past few years. It means the surveillance of a person's private activities, meetings, movements and conversations designed in such a way that the person concerned is unaware of the surveillance. The only form of such surveillance covered by statutory law in Hong Kong had been the interception of telecommunications, by virtue of the Telecommunications Ordinance. Another statute, the Interception of Communications Ordinance, passed in 1997, has never been brought into effect. Besides these, there are also standing orders in the various law enforcement agencies restricting the use of this means to obtain evidence. In the case of *R v Li Man Tak* (2005), the constitutionality of evidence obtained in such a manner without being 'in accordance with the law' was challenged, and was judged to be unlawful. In both this case and the further case of *R v Shum Chiu* (2005), Article 30 of the Basic Law, which guarantees the basic right to privacy, was put to the fore. The Chief Executive subsequently issued the 'Law Enforcement (Covert Surveillance) Procedures Order' in July 2005 detailing the procedures for lawful authorisation of covert surveillance. However, as its name suggests, the Order only applies in the case of law enforcement agencies such as the Independent Commission against Corruption (ICAC). In any case, the constitutionality of the Order, an administrative direction rather than law in the strict sense, remains doubted by authorities.

On 6 August 2006, at the end of a record-setting 57½-hour legislative session, the Hong Kong Legislative Council passed the Interception of Communications and Covert Surveillance Bill. Briefly, we have incorporated the key safeguards of judicial oversight and a specially created commissioner to oversee the approval and use of electronic surveillance. The new Ordinance regulates essentially law enforcement officials entering an individual's premises or office secretly to install listening devices.

The above, therefore, have no application in our scenario. Our case is not one of covert surveillance at all. The laboratory assistant knew well about the monitoring. What could have come to her aid? The Personal Data (Privacy) Ordinance would not be relevant unless the monitoring was recorded, which would then amount to the 'processing' of the data, thus bringing the matter within the remits of the Ordinance. However, even if that were the case, the Ordinance does not prevent such collection of data when done in consistency with the data collection principles in Schedule 1, in being fair and lawful for purpose, informed, subject to rights of usage at collection, and access, etc.

Ultimately, one therefore has to come to the **human rights** issue. The English Human Rights Act 1998 was enacted in order to bring home to the United Kingdom the principles of the European Convention of Human Rights so that it became no longer necessary to take cases all the way to the Court of Human Rights in Strasbourg. No 'Human Rights Ordinance' was, however, passed in Hong Kong. Nevertheless, the principles of the European Convention still enshrine, though somewhat indirectly, as they are regarded and referred to as a standard benchmark in the courts. Of particular relevance is Article 8 of the Convention. This article ensures an individual's right to private life subject only to lawful interference by a public body in the interests of national security, public safety and economic well-being of the country concerned; the prevention of disorder or crime; protection of health or morals; or the rights and freedom of others.

On the other hand, Article 17 of the International Covenant on Civil and Political Rights, incorporated into Hong Kong by the Hong Kong Bill of Rights 1991, provides that 'No one shall be subjected to arbitrary or **unlawful interference with his privacy**… ' and that 'everyone has the right to the protection of the law against such interference or attacks.' Furthermore, Article 39 of the Basic Law guarantees that 'The provisions of the International Covenant on Civil and Political Rights, the International Covenant on Economic, Social and Cultural Rights, and… shall remain in force.'

It can now be seen that the problem is highly complicated and technical. Furthermore, although there are grounds on which the one being scrutinised might base his or her case, it should not be forgotten that in any event it would be pretty expensive to pursue.

For the person who decides on monitoring, it is preferable to give prior warning of and the reasons for such a decision. Any monitoring instituted must be reasonable as to the manner of monitoring, be kept proportionate as to the degree of monitoring and be done with good justification.

References and Further Reading
1. Telecommunications Ordinance, Chapter 106 of the Laws of Hong Kong.

2. Interception of Communications and Surveillance Ordinance, Chapter 589 of the Laws of Hong Kong.

3. Yam K. *Covert surveillance by law enforcement agencies*. Hong Kong Lawyer, 2005; (09): 33-40.

4. *R v Li Man Tak* (2005) CAAR 1/2005.

5. *R v Shum Chiu* (2005) 1 HKLRD 155.

6. Kellogg TE. *A Flawed Effort? Legislating on Surveillance in Hong Kong*. Hong Kong Journal: the Quarterly Online Journal about Issues relating to Hong Kong and China 1/2007 available at www.hkjournal.org/archive/2007_summer/kellogg.htm.

7. Personal Data (Privacy) Ordinance, Chapter 486 of the Laws of Hong Kong.

8. English Human Rights Act 1998.

9. European Convention of Human Rights.

10. International Covenant on Civil and Political Rights of the United Nations 1966.

11. Hong Kong Bill of Rights 1991.

12. Article 39, Basic Law of the HKSAR.

13. International Covenant on Economic, Social and Cultural Rights of the United Nations 1966.

14. *Privacy: The Regulation of Covert Surveillance.* The Law Reform Commission of Hong Kong 2006.

15. *Civil Liability for Invasion of Privacy*. The Law Reform Commission of Hong Kong 2004.

43

A bad reference

It is a matter of routine to request a reference from one's superior at work when applying for a new post, such as an appointment to a more senior position in an institution. A reference can and often does affect success in the new appointment. However, a reference can also be inaccurate, incomplete, or maliciously written to be **misleading**.

Where someone receives a bad reference the contents of which he or she disagrees with, is there a remedy? What if the employer refuses to write the reference altogether?

The usual first step is to see if there is an element of **sex discrimination** which might allow a cause of action. This sidesteps the issue but is actually a common and powerful means of seeking a remedy.

The next option, then, is to look for elements pointing to a possibility of libel, i.e. **defamation**. However, it can be very difficult to prove that the contents of a reference are wrong and the legal costs may be prohibitive as such litigations are often protracted.

Apart from these approaches, the more often taken course nowadays is based on the landmark case of *Spring v Guardian Assurance plc* (1994). The House of Lords in this case decided that an employer in providing a reference is under a duty to the employee and the prospective employer to take reasonable care to ensure that the contents of the reference are fair, accurate and balanced. Such an employer can be liable in **negligence** for any economic loss that the employee or the prospective employer suffers as a result. An employee can thus pursue the employer for damages arising in relation to or out of the 'bad' report if he can prove the negligence of the employer and that that negligence is casually related to his loss.

However, the employer can refuse to write the reference from the start if that is the practice of the organisation or if he is consistent in refusing to do so for all employees. There is usually no way to insist upon a reference in such a situation unless there has been a prior contractual agreement to provide a reference, but that is rare.

One minor point of interest in this connection is whether the employee has the **right to look** at the contents of the reference. Such right would and only would arise where the employee is successful in his new job and applies then to obtain a copy of the report under the Personal Data (Privacy) Ordinance. An employer should therefore note that the contents of a reference are not strictly confidential as they disclose personal information which fits into the meaning of personal data under that ordinance.

References and Further Reading

1.   *Spring v Guardian Assurance plc* (1994) 2 AC 296.
2.   Personal Data (Privacy) Ordinance, Chapter 486 of the Laws of Hong Kong.
3.   *Writing References*. General Medical Council 2007 at GMC website under the List of Ethical Guidance at http://www.gmc-uk.org/guidance/current/library/writing_references.asp.

I want to see Dr. X!

Not uncommonly in public hospital settings patients returning for follow-up request to see a particular doctor. If that particular doctor is around and on duty, quite often we allow them the convenience. On the other hand, do patients have such a right in the first place?

The answer obviously depends on whether the scenario is one which concerns a private institution or clinic, or whether it is the public service. In the private sector, the customer is always right as they are the source of your income. In the public hospitals, however, this is not the case although the trend is to look upon the provided service in a business sense and customer satisfaction is emphasised.

Strictly speaking, a **public patient** is public. This means that he is a patient of the Hospital Authority. The doctor employees are agents of the principal, i.e. the Authority, and carry out medical treatment on its behalf. The relationship is between the patient and the Authority.

Having said that, the doctor is a highly respected professional in society and the patient confers upon him trust and confidence. It is therefore also difficult to argue that the doctor concerned should not do his best to serve the requesting patient if at all feasible. Nevertheless, it is equally correct to say that an unreasonable demanding patient need not be entertained.

The conclusion is that the patient has no absolute right to demand seeing any particular doctor. If the particular doctor is available and pleased to do so, he has the discretion whether to entertain the request or not.

Orders from your boss to which you disagree!

This is more a **politics** exercise and is indeed a very sensitive topic. What should one do and how should one respond in this difficult situation?

The possibilities are four:

	Boss Right	Boss Wrong
You Right	A	B
You Wrong	C	D

Situations A and D are uncommon.

Situation B is also unlikely as your boss should have better experience.

Therefore, the usual case is of a Situation C scenario. The answer is then straightforward and obvious. Listen and think thrice before a protest is made. Go back and research. Obtain further third party advice. No hurried reaction is advisable. Do not forget that although the boss may be wrong, he thinks that he is right.

The author has this story to tell. When he was a house officer and on call one evening in his teaching hospital, a construction site worker was admitted through the Casualty Department, as it was then called (nowadays the Accident and Emergency). He had a splinter injury with a tiny piece of iron lodged in the (R) cheek and confirmed on plain X-ray. The patient was perfectly well apart from a 3mm cheek laceration, caused by the splinter entry. This was the first time the author had come across this kind of injury, but the man was immediately taken to the dressing room for exploration of the wound. After a full hour of self-torture under the poor lighting provided by a mah-jong lamp, the intense summer heat and humidity of a room without air conditioning, an aching back and neck from assuming an unnatural posture for a too-low couch when standing and a too-high one when sitting, and a patient who was yelling and cursing, it was time to seek help. Despite much difficulty in shouting for assistance from the nurse at the distant station outside, she came and was kind enough to agree to page my first call for help. The answer was, however, 'ask him to close it up' and that he would not be coming along. 'Page the second on-call,' I begged, but the answer was the same. Swearing that I would not be coming back there for training, I ungloved to page the third call myself. This kind and careful gentleman answered promptly without a single hesitation and said he would come immediately. When he arrived, he took a casual look at the patient's cheek and asked the nurse to get the suture material he wanted. The next thing he did was to close up the wound.

I was immediately puzzled because he seemed to have been a conscientious physician and yet he was now doing something contradictory and not showing any diligence in the search.

When he finished, he explained that in most cases there is no need to retrieve the foreign body as it is practically always harmless. Until that moment, I was still struggling within myself as to how I should put the story of the two 'lazy' medical officers to him!

Your senior is usually right!

46

Authorship in publications

In the not too distant past, it was not uncommon to think that more authors were better when submitting scientific papers. You have more friends who may include you next time in their work. You please your seniors. Your paper seems more important because it is a collaborative work.

At the same time, there were indeed practitioners who thought that since the material of the work belonged to the Department, the Department heads deserved to have their names on the paper, and demanded so.

This is bad as it confuses who the real contributors are. In a more critical sense, it is dishonest if authors are included who have contributed nothing but a signature.

Guidelines on authorship have existed for decades but they are not always followed consistently. There have been incentives for name inclusion as suggested above.

The Vancouver Convention was described by the International Committee of Medical Journal Editors (ICMJE) in the 1980s. Under this system, authorship requires '**substantial contribution**' to either: conception and design; acquisition of data; or analysis and interpretation of data; and drafting or revising and the final approval of the script. In particular, funding and general supervision are not sufficient criteria for authorship.

In the past decade, new standards for authorship have been put forward, notably by Professor Paul Friedman from the Council of Science Editors. The main theme is to include a detailed list of author contributions based on criteria like conception of project, design of study, supervision, resources acquisition, provision of study materials, data collection and processing, analysis and interpretation of data, literature search, script writing, critical review, etc. It was suggested that at least two or three of the listed criteria are required for authorship. Persons who contributed in only one category are to be acknowledged. Such **declarations of responsibility** aim at a better identification of the contributions from individual authors.

The new system has been variably used by a number of journals. Since 1997, the Lancet has been using this authorship contribution format, followed by the British Medical Journal in 1998. However, the 'substantial contribution' criteria are still used more widely as the basis for most journals.

It is not always a blessing to enjoy 'free' inclusion of one's name in a publication. A good example is the infamous South Korean stem cell debacle related to the cloning researcher Woo Suk Hwang who published two articles in Science in 2004 and 2005. Hwang claimed that his laboratory at the Seoul National University had successfully extracted stem cells from cloned human embryos, which later proved to be false. A co-author of the 2005 article, a renowned American stem-cell research authority, was subsequently involved in an allegation of research misbehaviour for failing to more closely oversee research with his name on it.

Similar fraudulent publications have been said to have happened locally and it cannot be over-emphasised that rights as well as responsibilities are inherent in the name of an author.

References and Further Reading

1. International Committee of Medical Journal Editors website at: http://www.icmje.org/.
2. Council of Science Editors website at: http://www. councilscienceeditors.org/.
3. Alliance for Human Research Protection website at: http://www. ahrp.org/cms/content/view/29/29/.
4. Hwang WS et al. *Patient-specific embryonic stem cells derived from human SCNT blastocysts.* Science 2005; 308: 1777-1783.

47

Unauthorised use of the hospital computer system

Equipment is provided in employment for the performance of duties at work. There are a number of rules regulating the use of such equipment. The area that we go into here is the opposite: the misuse of such equipment by the employee.

One example is the provision of computers in hospitals for work. Are there restrictions as to the use we put them to? The answer is a clear yes. Justification for the rules is obvious. The computers are there for one or more purposes related to the institution's work. They are not there for personal affairs. Use of such for undesignated purposes is thus only justifiable if the computer is personally designated for individual deployment. Perhaps even in the latter situation there is still an implied obligation to restrict the use to work-related duties.

Why are we so concerned whether it is authorised use or not? The key lies in the liability resulting from **unauthorised use** causing damage either to the system or therefrom.

If the reader is not convinced, an example will illustrate the point. Imagine a staff member downloading material from unsafe websites which results in the installation of spyware or viruses in the hospital's system. If it causes loss of patients' records or leakage of patient data, whose responsibility is it?

The scope of improper usage of computer systems goes beyond visiting websites unrelated to work. Strictly speaking, using the messaging system for communication with personal friends, installation of software not authorised, downloading of information without permission, or even merely using the system to produce printouts not related to work are acts which could potentially attract liability.

At the very minimum, a colleague who commits such a mischief can potentially be subject to internal enquiry and penalty depending on the institution's standing regulations.

48

Avoiding complaints

Complaints are annoying. Complaints are disgusting. Complaints are distressing. Complaints are insulting. Complaints are disheartening.

Honestly, no one wants complaints, although modern management theories see complaints as 'opportunities for improvement'. Certainly, if a doctor receives complaints all the time, the supervisors will be wondering what is wrong with that doctor.

Can we avoid complaints? The answer is perhaps not too encouraging because it is no. A complaint is basically something arising out of a mutual relationship between two parties. You can be prudent and professional. The other party, however, can always be insane and unreasonable.

But we can reduce the chances of being a victim of a complaint.

How?

The solution will be clear if one is to first look into the reasons why patients file complaints. Patients complain because they are unhappy with something. If the subject of their complaint is you as a doctor, then they are unhappy with you.

'Why should a patient be unhappy with me?' one may immediately ask.

According to information derived from a vast number of cases handled by the Medical Protection Society, very often there is already some disappointment with the doctor-patient interaction on the part of the patient. This may be due to the doctor being too much in a hurry, having not addressed the patient's main concerns, having not shown empathy, or having not given the patient sufficient chance to voice his worries, etc. These are predisposing factors for complaints. The result is that the patient is not pleased with the doctor concerned. He or she may even be angry at the doctor. Yet it often takes more than simply an unsatisfactory encounter for the patient to take action.

What triggers the outburst is a precipitating event. Examples of such are a known complication occurring, a minor mistake on the part of the medical personnel, a slight confusion of arrangements caused by miscommunication between colleagues affecting the patient, etc. One or more of these is enough to cause the patient to speak out and take the case to the hospital's patient relations manager. Under ordinary circumstances, these latter events are not really significant enough to set anything in motion nor would they be sufficient to warrant any litigation. However, they have now become instrumental in causing a disaster because the patient had been 'prepared'. They are the straw which breaks the camel's back.

How to avoid this situation now becomes clear. To reduce the risk of a medical practitioner being the subject of a complaint, spend more effort in developing a better doctor-patient relationship.

Some doctors will question why if they have been very nice to a patient, the patient is still unhappy with them. The answer here is that it is not the doctor's perception but that of the patient which counts. A medical practitioner therefore has to be very sensitive and tailor his behaviour to the 'needs' of the patient.

We keep on hearing stories of forgiving patients despite their having been on the receiving end of a clinical error. Studies indeed have shown that complaints and legal action are most often not made or taken against negligent doctors but against those whom patients were not happy with. Quite logically, if patients are pleased with you and are thankful, they will not at the same time think of challenging or harming you.

The culture of modern medical care has changed from what it used to be. It is not wrong to say that concepts of consumerism have superseded paternalism. A team-based approach is emphasised and heroic individualism is no longer in vogue. We nowadays constantly review our policies and standard teachings with evidence-based data to guide our decisions. We treat our errors positively and make improvements instead of hiding and covering them up. We investigate problems to fix them rather than assigning blame.

One aspect of the doctor's practice has remained unchanged. In an article in the Surgical News of the Australasian College of Surgeons, a medical insurance group advised on good medico-legal risk management and emphasised that 'good old-fashioned etiquette never goes astray'. Five Cs were raised as important in reducing risk: competence, culture, communication, courtesy and candour. Competence, often taken to be the only factor of importance by many more experienced doctors, is just one of the five.

The author has a real story to tell. A doctor who was working in the same department years back once performed a hernia repair on the wrong side. Those were the days when there was still nothing like a surgical checklist before putting a patient to sleep. The 'unfortunate' doctor was very worried. What made things worse was that the elderly patient went on to develop postoperative bronchopneumonia and his condition deteriorated a little more each day. What could one have done apart from praying and doing whatever possible medically? The young doctor talked to the relatives at length each day and was honest about what had happened. He explained, counselled, provided support, showed empathy, did what he could have done and repeatedly did so. To be frank, I was not really sure if the doctor's motive was one of genuine kindness and good or whether he was merely putting on a show. What was in no doubt was the end result when the old gentleman passed away. To the surprise of every member of the department, a thank-you card was sent to the chief in honour of the young doctor who had been the very wrongdoer from the start. The relatives were so grateful for the treatment received they disregarded the mistake!

References and Further Reading

1. Paul Nisselle. *Medico-legal risk management*. Surgical News of the Royal Australasian College of Surgeons 2009; 10(6): 41.

2. Ambady N, LaPlante D et al. *Surgeon's tone of voice: a clue to malpractice history.* Surgery 2002; 132(1): 5-9.

3. Hobma S, Ram P et al. *Effective improvement of doctor-patient communication: a randomized controlled trial.* Br J Gen Pract 2006; 56(529): 580-587.

4. Vincent C, Young M et al. *Why do people sue doctors? A study of patients and relatives taking legal action.* Lancet 1994; 343: 1609-1613.

49

Accepting gifts and presents

Doctors, as a result of their work, often win appreciation from patients and relatives. Sometimes this is in the form of gifts and presents. As they are personal, why can't we just take them, as is often said?

The reason is that we have to stay clear from any hint of accepting a bribe, or at the least, any conflict of interest.

What is meant by bribery? Bribery is defined in detail in the Prevention of Bribery Ordinance (Chapter 201 of the Laws of Hong Kong) sections 3 to 10 to which the reader is referred. Briefly, it is the acceptance or offer of an advantage in exchange for some performance or abstinence from performance, or expediting, delaying, hindering or preventing, any act; or assisting or favouring anyone, in one's capacity at work as a public servant, or in the private sector, in relation to one's principal's business, in the absence of any lawful authority or reasonable excuse.

The word 'advantage' is obviously critical. Advantage is defined in section 2 of the Ordinance, and can be valuables, office, employment, contract, a discharge of obligation, service, a favour, protection from penalty, or the exercise or forbearance from exercise of any right.

It would then at first sound simple to everyone what exactly bribery is. However, one can quickly see from the above that the definition is indeed very wide and if one is not on the alert, it is not difficult to fall inadvertently within the technical boundaries of the statute.

Why should we doctors be concerned in the first instance? Well, the answer is that there are many situations where there are potential dangers. Examples would include unequal treatment of some patients, preferential referral to certain laboratories, choice of certain pharmaceutical products, accepting sponsorships from drug firms, acceptance of a donation, acceptance of a particular contract, and many more.

What can we do to stay safe then? A few general principles can be stated to reduce the risk of falling within the definition of bribery. First, avoid the acceptance of any advantage. Second, if that is not avoidable, declare and let the principal, i.e. employer, know as soon as possible of it. The latter is provided by the statute itself as leeway but is not applicable if one is in the position of a government servant working for the HKSAR, to which more stringent rules pertain. Third, be ready to justify choices and preferences with real, valid and lawful reasons. Fourth, do not accept the offer personally but direct it to the department or institution as the beneficiary. Fifth, ask yourself whether you would feel obliged to offer anything in return as a result of accepting the advantage. Any answer in the affirmative would signal a halt to any acceptance. Sixth, ask whether the acceptance would pass the 'sunshine test', meaning that if it were to be disclosed to all concerned, would it raise suspicion from any of the parties involved or others.

After considering all the above, what is right and what is wrong are perhaps often a matter of commonsense.

It is, however, also important to take note of section 11. Section 11 states that it is not a defence if the promised act was not performed, never intended to be performed, or was not in the capacity of the agent to perform. This means that accepting an advantage as an inducement and claiming that there was no actual genuine intention to offer something in return is not a valid excuse. One cannot be too wise here! The reaching of an agreement, albeit merely verbal, is enough to contravene the law.

Another point worth noting is the exception of 'entertainment' from the definition of advantage. Entertainment means the provision of food or drink for immediate consumption on the spot. It is therefore alright if a pharmaceutical company sponsors the provision of some snacks and refreshment for the whole department when presenting a new product during a department meeting, for example. For the same reason, the provision of gifts to be taken away would be an advantage because it would be outside the scope of entertainment.

Yet one further point about the definition of advantage is that there is no minimal value or worth to an advantage, as is often thought to be the case. The lowest value involved in Hong Kong's history is often said to be a case involving a sum of only HK$5, which was demanded by a minor staff member in a government hospital in return for provision of the service which she was instructed to give to a patient. The lesson from this would be that red packets at the Lunar New Year or small gifts or presents as items of appreciation are better avoided, unless there are provisions in the institution's policy authorising their acceptance and that the stipulations and procedures have been followed.

Lastly, medical practitioners should know the burden of proof under section 24 for the purposes of this particular Ordinance. Section 24 stipulates that 'In any proceedings against a person for an offence under this Ordinance, the burden of proving a defence of lawful authority or reasonable excuse shall lie upon the accused.' The clear-thinking doctor should now be aware that this is the opposite of the usual rule where it is the burden of the prosecution to prove that the defendant is guilty. In practice, this means that it is always better and safer to avoid any hint of corruptive conduct.

References and Further Reading

1. Prevention of Bribery Ordinance (Chapter 201 of the Laws of Hong Kong).
2. *Integrity in Practice: A Practical Guide for Medical Practitioners on Corruption Prevention*. ICAC and HKMA.

50

Internet medical practice

Increasingly, the internet is becoming an integral part of the life of the modern citizen. Communication, in particular, has been radically revolutionalised in the past decade. Never before in mankind's recorded history has there been seen such speed and long-distance dissemination of information.

The development of the internet is definitely bringing with it implications for the practice of medicine. Thus, many colleagues are receiving e-mails seeking advice from new potential patients. Others are creating websites for their practice or clinics. There are agents soliciting medical practitioners to enrol in their listings to attract patients. There are even vendors seeking to design web pages for doctors with the aim of attracting business. Even drugs can easily be available over the web at reduced costs.

What are the legal implications of all these new developments that we medical practitioners should take note of?

It would seem at first sight that we are venturing into something entirely novel and, with the lack of precedents, it might be difficult to know what the rules are or whether one is at liberty to do what one likes, taking advantage of the state of affairs.

In actual fact, however, the guiding principles are not at all that difficult to derive. There is simply no reason why our existing ethical principles should not apply to the internet scenario. The Code of Professional Conduct published by the Medical Council of Hong Kong is a collection of the principles at hand. Obviously, the Code is not to be taken piecemeal because the spirit behind the black and white of the plain English is the more important message. Thus, one can, with a little diligence, pick out the relevant sections which would dictate our behaviour in the web milieu.

The important messages from these sections are:

- No misleading advertisement and no practice promotion (5.1.3).
- Information provided must be accurate, factual, objectively verifiable, and balanced (5.2.1.1); not exaggerated or misleading, or claim superiority or uniqueness without justifications. No solicitation or canvassing; no commercial promotion; not be sensational or unduly persuasive; not arousing unjustified concern or distress; not generate unrealistic expectations; and not disparage other doctors (5.2.1.2).
- No practice promotion for an individual doctor or his group (5.2.1.3).
- Information may be made available to the public as stipulated only (5.2.3.5).
- Service information dissemination to patients should not involve intrusive visits, unsolicited calls, or mails; exerting undue pressure; or offering guarantees; or taking advantage of one's professional capacity to promote or sell medical products (5.2.4.2 and 5.2.5).
- No disguised practice promotion under the cloak of health education (6).
- No disguised practice promotion under the cloak of health organisation advertisements (18.1 and 18.2).

A report published by the Federation of State Medical Boards of the United States in 2002 on online care emphasised the importance of placing patients first, maintaining standards, ethics, supervision and protecting confidentiality. It underlined that the duty of care starts with the physician agreeing to undertake diagnosis and treatment. Guidelines were established for medical practitioners using the internet in the delivery of patient care:

- Patients must be carefully evaluated.
- Treatment offered must be to the same standard as conventional care, e.g. prescription should not be based solely on an online questionnaire.
- Written policies should be in place, e.g. privacy, personnel involved, hours of operation, transactions permitted, required patient information, security and quality assurance.
- Written informed consent should be maintained, including harmless clause for loss of data.
- Medical records should be filed.
- Security measures for patient confidentiality should be in place, e.g. password protection, encryption and authentication.
- Disclosure of the medical practice, e.g. ownership, provided services, office address, contact information, physician qualifications, fees and payment, appropriate usage, information handling and patients' rights.
- Links to health sites are permitted.

It is a fact that legislation and case law currently lag behind the rapidly advancing technological changes worldwide.

The author may be old fashioned and a little stubborn but has always some hesitation in entertaining cold unsolicited enquiries from persons who purport to be seeking medical advice. At best, it is the author's opinion that an appointment should be offered to such persons and a formal conventional consultation be initiated. We are of course talking about medical practice here in Hong Kong. Regardless of the worry of misunderstandings occurring through non-verbal communication, it is without doubt difficult to imagine deriving any real clinical sense without even touching the patient. The giving of anything but general comments is not advisable lest a wrong or inappropriate remark be made in a written form. In any case, it could be very difficult to maintain that due care had been exercised in the face of a later claim of professional negligence when conclusions have been drawn without even 'seeing' the patient. There is also the further danger of prescribing medication and the selling of dangerous drugs without a reliable means of proof of the identity of the 'patient' or the real existence of the problems.

Having said all this, the young medical practitioner should anticipate the arrival of this new modality of practice in the future and should be on the lookout for relevant regulations and changes.

References and Further Reading

1. *Model Guidelines for the Appropriate Use of the Internet in Medical Practice*. Federation of State Medical Boards of the United States, Inc. 2002.
2. Sara Williams. *Tangled web*. Casebook (Asia). Medical Protection Society 2009; 17(2): 8-11.
3. Paragraphs 5, 6 and 18, Code of Professional Conduct of the Medical Council of Hong Kong.

51

Distant medical technology

An interesting aspect of modern communication which has a potentially serious impact on how medical practice is conducted is the use of telemedicine. Telemedicine is the application of telecommunication technology to provide medical information and services. Teleradiology and telepathology are becoming fashionable in some quarters and these involve the transmission of stored information to and fro. Real-time face-to-face video conferencing, on the other hand, allows the opportunity for discussion among professionals. It might not be long therefore before medical consultation for patients takes place employing the latter platform.

How does one come to terms with this new situation? The point here is that the manner in which medical consultation is conducted is 'conventional' rather than that which is conducted via e-mails and photographic images sent over the internet. There are face-to-face verbal interactions with videoconferencing and a lot of the worries and uncertainties are done away with.

As far as the present day ethical standard in Hong Kong is concerned, under the Code of Professional Conduct of the Medical Council of Hong Kong a doctor can publish certain details of his practice on a website (5.2.3.5). The service information allowed is that permitted on doctors' directories under 5.2.3.7. The guidelines for doctors' directories are found in the Code in Appendix D.

Again, a number of guidelines are already available on the web from several western countries. The essence of these guidelines emphasises the importance of the following issues:

- Practitioners must be authorised to practise medicine in their country. With direct patient practice, he or she must also be authorised to practise in the state where the patient is normally resident or the service must be internationally approved;
- Doctors and patients must be able to reliably identify each other in a telemedicine consultation;
- Direct patient consultation should be restricted to where a doctor cannot be physically present within acceptable time. The doctor should have an existing professional relationship with the patient;
- A doctor consulting another doctor's advice remains responsible for treatment and decisions;
- A doctor performing medical interventions via telemedical techniques is responsible for those interventions;
- Equipment necessary must be of a sufficiently high standard and adequately operational;
- Medical opinions and recommendations should only be made with sufficient relevant information of the necessary quality and quantity;
- Interventions over a distance must be offered only where there are adequately trained personnel to continue care;
- Adequate patient records and documentation must be maintained;
- Medical ethics, patient consent and confidentiality principles are to be observed.

Telemedicine is an effective way to adequately utilise available human and material resources through advances in modern communication technology. Its role in the practice of medicine will certainly be assuming a much greater importance in the not too distant future.

References and Further Reading

1. *Ethical Guidelines in Telemedicine.* Executive Board of the Finnish Medical Association 1997.
2. Telemedicine Standards and Guidelines. American Telemedicine Association at http://www.americantelemed.org.
3. Robert Milstein. Chapter 5: *Duty of Care, Standard of Care and Standards* in *Report on Telemedicine: An international comparative analysis of policy, regulatory and medico-legal obstacles and solutions.* Department of Human Services (State of Victoria) 1999.
4. Paragraph 5 and Appendix D, Code of Professional Conduct of the Medical Council of Hong Kong.

II

Consent

——— 52 ———

A valid consent

Everyone knows that it is now necessary to obtain consent from patients before procedures are undertaken. The topic has been hotly debated for a number of years for a variety of reasons. Let us reflect on certain questions.

Why is consent relevant anyway? The answer is simple. Everyone is entitled to the fundamental human right of autonomy over what can be done to one's body. This right is as basic as a mere touching of the body of a person. This is no exaggeration. We increasingly see newspaper reports of indecent assault on the underground. Many of these cases involve merely the touching of another person's body, obviously without consent.

In law, a mere touching is sufficient to constitute **battery**. Even a verbal insult without touching could be an **assault**. So why should a patient be deprived of his or her right to this autonomy over the control of his or her body when in front of a doctor? A doctor is therefore not right in law to do even the necessary to obtain a diagnosis or give treatment without valid consent from the patient.

Do we have to get consent before we touch patients for the purpose of doing a physical examination in the consultation room? Strictly the answer is yes. It may be presumed that the patient by coming to the consultation freely and of his own volition has given **implied consent** for examination. That is correct and is usually the basis to go ahead without further confirmation. However, it is good medical practice to begin a sensitive step with something like, 'I am going to examine your breasts, is that OK?'

What is a **valid consent** then? Many medico-legal disputes are related to whether consent given was valid. A mere written signature is only evidence of a possibly valid consent, not exactly a valid consent per se. To be valid, consent needs to consist of the following elements to be understood by the patient:

- The procedure that is to be done;
- The nature of the procedure;
- The risks and benefits of the procedure;
- Alternative options available and their risks and benefits;
- The effects and consequences of non-treatment;
- Any information related to the particular circumstances specific to the patient.

There must also be no invalidating factors.

How much in terms of depth and width is needed is a question often posed by the defensive young doctor in the face of instructions for how a proper consent should be obtained. The concept that is relevant here is that of **informed consent**. By informed consent we mean that sufficient details are given so as to enable a patient to arrive at a reasoned decision.

The elements under the bullet points above are also the areas where patients and their lawyers can focus their attack(s). Specifically they have the burden of proving one or more of these features is/are deficient or lacking. The doctor may then have to prove that they are not.

What are the **invalidating factors**? They include:

- consent not given under free will, e.g. with coercion or undue influence; and,
- consent given by someone mentally incapable in the law, e.g. a minor, the mentally insane or handicapped, or someone in a state of confusion.

A minor or an infant in law is one who is less than 18 years of age (section 2 of the Age of Majority (Related Provisions) Ordinance). The context, though, has to be looked at and the reader is referred to the chapter on *Gillick*-competence. For the mentally incapacitated, the guardian will be able to provide consent (Mental Health Ordinance, section 59ZD). Furthermore, treatment of the mentally handicapped may be carried out without consent if it is in their best interest in an emergency situation and if it appears that no guardian was appointed, or if the guardian was not conferred the power to give consent (Mental Health Ordinance, section 59ZE and 59ZE).

Obtaining valid consent is not to be looked at as a troublesome routine for the prudent medical practitioner. The busy doctor is often found to scribble a mere word or two, possibly just the diagnosis and the name of the procedure, on a pre-printed consent form and no more. This is dangerous practice in addition to being irresponsible. The consent form is there actually to offer protection both for the doctor and the patient. It ensures that patients have been given the necessary information to make a well-balanced decision for themselves; it protects the doctor from allegations of not having provided material information to enable that process. Quite simply anything not recorded **in written form** is presumed not mentioned and a doctor might have a hard time proving that it had been mentioned, without any guarantee of success.

Do we need to mention all possible outcomes and consequences and write a volume to enumerate the latter? No. The court looks at what is **reasonable**. Certainly a safe course of action for the doctor would be for him to put himself in the position of the patient and consider what information is necessary to reach a well-balanced decision. Along the same vein, a brief word or two on each important point is good evidence that something has been mentioned.

What is meant by **particular circumstances** specific to a particular patient? An example will illustrate the point. A 75-year-old lady comes to you having sustained a fall at home resulting in a depressed cheek prominence from an underlying fracture in the zygoma. As a plastic surgeon you can easily fix this with an operation. The specific point to mention here would be that the procedure is purely cosmetic in the absence of functional impairment. The reason for this is that an elderly lady may not regard cosmetic restoration as sufficiently vital to warrant general anaesthesia. The young and active patient, on the other hand, would not even consider that point as relevant as deformed facial features could be detrimental in their future careers. The best approach to ensure that information which is necessary in particular circumstances is given is to ask the patient: 'Is there any question you wish to ask?'

It is becoming more customary in many institutions to use **pre-printed pamphlets** to convey information for the purpose of obtaining valid consents. This is a preferred approach but the medical practitioner should note that pamphlets are helpful in validating consent only if their contents are explained to the patient. It is prudent to document that an explanation was also given. It goes without saying that patients would otherwise be able to go back and claim that they did not understand what was written on the pamphlet and understood something else when signing. It is also good practice to add tick marks on the pamphlets point by point after the explanation, and finally to include the date and the signatures of both the doctor and the patient.

References and Further Reading

1. Age of Majority (Related Provisions) Ordinance, Chapter 410 of the Laws of Hong Kong.
2. Mental Health Ordinance, Chapter 136 of the Laws of Hong Kong.
3. *Gillick v West Norfolk and Wisbech Area Health Authority* (1984) QB 581.
4. *Guide to Doctors/Dentists: Consent to Medical and Dental Treatment of Mentally Incapacitated Person in the Context of Part IVB & Part IVC, Mental Health Ordinance (Cap. 136).* Guardianship Board of Hong Kong 2006.
5. *Consent to Medical and Dental Treatment.* Guardianship Board of Hong Kong 2005.

53

Age for consent: Gillick competence

A minor in law in Hong Kong is one who has not attained the age of 18 (Age of Majority (Related Provisions) Ordinance, section 2).

Imagine a 15-year-old girl, i.e. a **minor** in law, coming into your clinic one day asking for advice on contraception. You may or may not approve of sexual activity at that age but, in the event, what would you do?

You may denounce the conduct on immoral grounds. But do you inform the police? Do you inform the parents? Sexual intercourse with a girl under 16 is a crime in the law irrespective of whether there is consent. Would the doctor be regarded as an **accomplice** in the crime in facilitating illegal sex? Would refusal to give the advice perhaps do more harm than good in '**procuring**' an unwanted pregnancy? What about the duty of **confidentiality** to the patient here?

This scenario really happened in the United Kingdom in the case of *Gillick v West Norfolk and Wisbech Area Health Authority* (1984). The Department of Health published a circular stating that doctors could, in certain circumstances, give contraceptive advice to minors without parental consent. Mrs. Gillick, upon learning that her daughter was receiving such advice, sought to sue the Department and to obtain a declaration from the court that the instruction was unlawful. The case went all the way to the House of Lords and the Department of Health, backed by the British Medical Association, won.

The court considered that there are mature minors, now widely referred to as '*Gillick*-competent' girls, who are capable of giving consent for themselves despite being minors. The court also considered that a doctor in such a position would not be taken as abetting illegal

139

sexual intercourse unless that was his real intention. This is because an accessory to a crime must know the material circumstances of the offence, and not merely that sexual intercourse might take place at some unidentified future time with an unidentified man!

The message for the medical practitioner is that provided he is satisfied objectively that a minor under 16 years of age is ***Gillick-competent***, the minor's consent is valid and her confidentiality should be respected. In the assessment, the salient points are the child's capacity to understand the nature, purpose and possible consequences of an investigation or treatment, or the consequences of non-treatment.

In the case of minors between the ages of 16 and 18, it is generally regarded that they can be treated as adults and can be presumed to have the capacity to decide for themselves.

It may be of interest to note in passing that, congruent to our everyday impression of earlier intellectual development in children in general these days, the courts are also giving regard to this phenomenon. Thus the previous requirement for proof of a child's personal knowledge that a crime with which he is related is 'seriously wrong' in order to confer liability was abolished in England in 1998 by the British Parliament.

In the same vein, a generally preferred view nowadays is for a child and his or her wishes to be respected in commensuration with his or her particular level of mental development.

Going back to the specific issue of providing contraceptives to minors under the age of 16, Lord Fraser, gave in the *Gillick* judgment the following set of guidelines, now named after him:

'A doctor can give contraceptive advice or treatment to a person under 16 with out parental consent, provided that the doctor is satisfied that:

- the young person will understand the advice;
- the young person cannot be persuaded to tell his or her parents or to allow the doctor to tell them that they are seeking contraceptive advice;

- the young person is likely to begin or continue having unprotected sex with or without contraceptive treatment;
- the young person's physical or mental health care are likely to suffer unless he or she receives contraceptive advice or treatment; and,
- it is in the young person's best interests to give contraceptive advice or treatment.'

References and Further Reading

1. Age of Majority (Related Provisions) Ordinance, Chapter 410 of the Laws of Hong Kong.
2. *Gillick v West Norfolk and Wisbech Area Health Authority* (1984) QB 581.
3. *0-18 Years: Guidance for all Doctors* (2007). General Medical Council.

54

Guardianship issues

First, here's a story to start this chapter. A junior colleague paged the author one Saturday morning. A frail, elderly gentleman with dementia who was totally dependent on his not so elderly wife was suspected, after an episode of facial herpes zoster, to have developed a cavernous sinus thrombosis. An urgent MRI scan was indicated but the wife was strongly opposed to it, probably a little upset with the husband and really wanting to follow a strategy of non-intervention to enable him to pass away peacefully. Recognising that something was wrong, the young doctor in showing great concern for the man's well-being was seeking advice as to what to do.

Obviously it is risky to go ahead without valid informed consent. At the same time, it is not perhaps the doctor's job to police all family matters.

What should be done? The obvious first step is of course to exercise one's **communication skills** by persuading the wife to change her mind with valid supporting reasons emphasising that the best interests of the patient should be her primary consideration. But what if the wife were stubborn?

First of all, a doctor can actually proceed without consent if it is urgent treatment necessary to save life or limb. He is also entitled to proceed in the case of non-urgent treatment if that is in the **best interests** of the patient provided that the patient really does not have the capacity to decide for himself. Here it may be advisable to seek urgent psychiatric opinion on the patient's actual mental capacity.

Second, some knowledge of guardianship will come to one's assistance. What is meant by guardianship? A guardian is a legally appointed person who is thus possessed of the legal power to decide for the person concerned important personal matters in his or her best interests. This power includes consent to certain medical treatments. **Seeking a guardianship order** will be helpful if a doctor is uncomfortable with proceeding with treatment without consent from the patient or his relatives. Sometimes this is necessary due to disagreement among the relatives who are not able to come to a consensus for the doctor. The duty of a guardian is to ensure for the person concerned that his best interests are guaranteed. Examples of a suitable guardian can be a relative, a close friend, a social worker, or the Director of Social Welfare. Application for guardianship is made by submitting the necessary forms together with the reports of two medical practitioners, one of whom must be an approved doctor for the purpose. There is provision for an expedited hearing in case of need.

A **court order** could be sought if a guardian unreasonably objects to treatment for the person concerned or if the doctor reasonably thinks that there is insurmountable resistance from relatives hindering the proper exercise of powers by the guardian.

References and Further Reading

1. Age of Majority (Related Provisions) Ordinance, Chapter 410 of the Laws of Hong Kong.
2. *Guide to Doctors/Dentists: Consent to Medical and Dental Treatment of Mentally Incapacitated Person in the Context of Part IVB & Part IVC, Mental Health Ordinance (Cap. 136).* Guardianship Board of Hong Kong 2006.
3. *Consent to Medical and Dental Treatment.* Guardianship Board of Hong Kong 2005.

55

Emergency treatment and consent

Consent is a prior necessity to treatment. That is a well-known and accepted standard practice. That is why we sign consent forms with patients before surgery, before interventional procedures and before we initiate anything other than the most basic investigation.

There is, however, an **exception** to the rule. This is where the circumstances are such that it is not feasible to get consent and yet it is necessary to take immediate action to save life or limb.

An example of such a situation would be an unconscious head injury patient with an epidural haematoma on CT scan when no relatives can be found. Another example would be a demented elderly patient with peritonitis requiring immediate laparotomy but whose relatives are all in mainland China.

The **justification** for the exception is that a medical practitioner acting in good faith in the best interests of the patient would presumably have received the patient's consent anyway had the patient actually been able to give consent. It should be noted that each and every of the conditions in this statement is immensely important and represents a restrictive condition-precedent for the licence to proceed.

There are often **standing guidelines** in various institutions as to what the usual practice in such situations would be. Steps are taken to protect staff and patients so that usually the additional signature of another independent doctor or the medical superintendent is required.

References and Further Reading

1. Kenyon Mason, Alexander McCall Smith, and Graeme Laurie. *Law and Medical Ethics*, 6th edn. LexisNexis Butterworths 2002; Chapter 10, pp 309-363.
2. *Consent: Patients and Doctors making decisions together.* General Medical Council 2008 at website under the List of Ethical Guidance at http://www.gmc-uk.org/guidance/ethical_guidance/consent_guidance/index.asp.

56

Is consent for treatment a contract?

The author once listened to a talk delivered by a chief of a hospital department on quality management in his department. He was drawing the relevance of the components of the ISO 2000 requirements to his clinical situation and was illustrating to the audience how useful the analogy was in the re-engineering of processes in his department. One interesting issue was his comment on 'contract making' in relation to the obtaining of consent in the medical context.

It is thus enlightening to examine if obtaining consent is a form of contracting.

To proceed any further, the reader will be aware that we need to know what is regarded as **a contract in law**. To be brief, the essence of a contract which would be accepted as such by the court would be an agreement which possesses the following characteristics:

- Offer by one party;
- Acceptance by the other party;
- Intention for the agreement to be legally binding;
- Consideration passing;
- Terms and obligations of the contract be clear.

In the presence of all these features, the agreement is said to be legally binding and will be enforceable if a party breaches the terms of the agreement.

To apply the above principles to the medical context of consent, it would seem that there is both **offer and acceptance**. This could be offer by the doctor to perform a procedure and acceptance of such by the patient. **Consideration** can be taken as the payment of a reasonable fee by the patient to the doctor. It goes without saying that there is an implied intention for the consent to be **legally binding**, or the doctor would be free to do anything he wishes, which is obviously not the case. As for the **terms of the agreement**, it is arguable that since the details of the procedure to be undertaken need to be explained and understood, including the alternatives, the benefits and risks, etc, the last criterion would also be satisfied.

In other words, giving consent does have the characteristics of a contract.

Having said this, it should not be taken that giving consent is totally equivalent to a contract because the two are entirely different in context. Consent is basically the giving of permission to the doctor for procedures which would otherwise amount to a battery on the body. Moreover, consent is not always necessary for treatment as happens in an emergency.

References and Further Reading

1. McKendrick E. *Contract Law*, 4th edn. Palgrave Law Masters 2000; Chapters 1-6.

———— 57 ————

Incidental surgery

When the author started his career in medicine in the early 80s, his surgeon-mentors used to perform incidental surgeries. By that is meant surgical procedures done on patients which are not exactly indicated or necessary.

To cite an example, if a patient labelled pre-operatively as having a perforated appendix turns out on laparotomy to have a perforated peptic ulcer, the surgeon might think that leaving the unaffected appendix behind would cause diagnostic confusion in future abdominal emergencies and he therefore removes that as well.

Strictly speaking, what was indicated during that scenario was a procedure for the peptic ulcer and the appendix was totally in a way a 'mere **innocent bystander**'. What was the right conferred upon the surgeon to remove a normal appendix? Do you give full and unrestricted licence to your doctor to do whatever he wants to do on your body by signing the consent form or are you agreeing to just a specific procedure?

There can be no excuse for incidental surgery unless that is **absolutely necessary**. Otherwise normal ovaries could be removed because they could be possible sites for future tumours or the uterus be removed because bleeding is not an uncommon cause for anaemia in women!

This does sometimes cause a dilemma. If a doctor were to encounter intra-operatively a situation where he has to do something additional to that included in the original consent, he may simply go ahead resting on **good faith**. The preferred approach in handling the difficulty, however, is not to be a brave surgeon but to contact the close relatives and discuss the issue with them. Concerned **understanding**

148

relatives who turn up at a phone call will in the experience of the author usually side with the doctor because they share common goals in the interests of the patient.

References and Further Reading

1.   Kenyon Mason, Alexander McCall Smith, and Graeme Laurie. *Law and Medical Ethics*, 6th edn. Butterworths 2002; Chapter 10, pp 309-363.

58

Clinical studies and patient consent

In the author's early days in the 80s, patients were not always recruited into trials with their prior knowledge. Many went through treatment without being aware that they had assisted in a clinical study. A personal example which the author can cite is a study which involved the testing of antibiotics for the prevention of wound infection after operation. Patients in different arms of the study received different drugs according to a random design. However, in reality some of the junior doctors picked through slips repeatedly until they found one for the drug which they thought was the most efficacious. This cheating was, at least initially, not to the knowledge of the chief investigator! It was therefore a really true 'double-blind'!

Those were the days! The world is more civilised now; not only is it widely accepted that patients have the **right to know** (and to refuse of course), the investigator also has an obligation to inform. The law of course does not touch upon this obligation directly unless there is damage from unauthentic or unaccepted forms of treatment. **Professional ethics**, here, however, is so overwhelmingly relevant that the medical community has now exercised self-discipline in a more conscientious manner both in medical research as well as in the management of patients.

Informed consent in this context would mean that patients are sufficiently informed so as to allow a rational decision to be made. Logically the details provided should include the options that are open, the advantages and risks of each, the experimental nature of particular options and their basis, and the likelihood of success with each. The medical practitioner must exercise his judgment here and the amount of information may well need to be tailored to the educational level and the intelligence of the particular patient. Very often a special research nurse or assistant is assigned the responsibility to recruit and provide explanation but the doctor concerned should always be at hand to offer further advice. Standard printout research protocols and forms are routine nowadays and they help ensure standardisation. Patients should be allowed time and opportunity to ask questions, to discuss the details with close relatives and to think things over. Consent in written form is practically mandatory.

The modern focus on patient-centred care explains why we have to seek prior approval from our own institution's Review Boards. Certification from such Boards are now a must in the submission of articles for publication whenever it comes to patient involvement.

Looking from this perspective, the young clinical investigator should feel proud of the profession to which he belongs in that it is upholding a high ethical standard. The review process is a checkpoint to ensure that our approaches are fair to patients and that patients are protected.

References and Further Reading

1. Kenyon Mason, Alexander McCall Smith, and Graeme Laurie. *Law and Medical Ethics*, 6th edn. LexisNexis Butterworths 2002; Chapter 19, pp 571-593.
2. *Research: The Role and Responsibilities of Doctors.* General Medical Council 2002 at GMC website under the List of Ethical Guidance at http://www.gmc-uk.org/guidance/current/library/research.asp.

59

Patient withdrawal of consent

Can patients withdraw their consent at the last moment?

There is no reason why not.

The basis of consent is a freewill agreement to something being done on one's body so as to confer **a restricted right** on the doctor to perform that which is agreed. As a result, so long as the patient of his own freewill thinks otherwise and wants to retract that right, he is fully entitled to do so at any point in time.

Once a clear withdrawal of consent is made, the right to intervene is immediately stopped from that specific point on. The former consent remains valid up to this point but it vanishes from then on.

The prudent practitioner may wish to document this, for the same reason as recording the details of consent, as evidence of the withdrawal of consent. However, even if the patient refuses to sign a refusal, if it is clearly the case that he is **no longer consenting**, the medical practitioner should immediately stop or finish off whatever is inevitable in relation to what he is doing to the patient.

One specific incidence of practical relevance of this principle in action is the patient who comes to the reception area of the operating theatre and suddenly decides that he or she does not want to have surgery. Despite the resultant disturbance to the operating schedule and the theatre, the surgeon will have no alternative but to cancel the case.

References and Further Reading

1. Kenyon Mason, Alexander McCall Smith, and Graeme Laurie. *Law and Medical Ethics*, 6th edn. LexisNexis Butterworths 2002; Chapter 10, pp 309-363.

III

Confidentiality

60

Data protection and privacy

Data protection and privacy have become very hot topics in the past few years and it is very important for members of the medical profession to grasp clearly the important concepts inherent in this area.

Privacy means the control of information revealing an individual or body. The concept without doubt is derived from the liberal-democratic cultures of the west where it is widely accepted that it is a basic human right to be left alone. Physical privacy refers to the freedom from intrusion into one's physical space in general; **informational privacy** means the right to access and correct collected data about oneself and the confidentiality associated with such data; and organisational privacy is related to secrets within institutions.

Of most relevance to the medical practitioner is informational privacy. This is because day in and day out information about patients is continuously being collected and filed, as written records are entered into computer systems. These are stored and are retrievable as patient identifiable data and are therefore governed by the Personal Data (Privacy) Ordinance.

In other words, in addition to the common law and ethical duty of confidentiality, there are clear statutory stipulations to ensure the collection, processing, storage, retrieval and use of data concerning identifiable individuals.

For this reason, apart from professional disciplinary actions against an offending medical practitioner, one has also to keep in mind the possibility of prosecution under the relevant provisions of the Ordinance by the Privacy Commissioner for Personal Data. This perhaps should cause sufficient alarm to the prudent medical practitioner in his handling of patient data.

The provisions of the Personal Data (Privacy) Ordinance can be read from the web as detailed in the Introduction to this work. Certain general principles in the security of patient data are in the sphere of responsibility of the medical practitioner. They are listed here for the convenience of colleagues as reminders of good practice:

- Do not download personal data unless absolutely necessary: Necessity is subject to the 'patient under care' and 'organisation need-to-know' principles.
- Always obey the data collection principles: Personal data should be collected lawfully and fairly, be accurate and kept up to date, be kept no longer than is necessary, be used only for the purposes collected, and data subjects ensured rights of access to and correction of the data.
- In the case of a good reason to justify keeping patient data in a mobile storage device: Always be discreet, keep the device very secure, and use encryption and passwords. It is easily overlooked that patient data can mean not only demographic and medical details but also clinical photos, research data and e-mail content concerning patients if the individuals are identifiable. It is also to be remembered that storage devices can include not only USBs but also laptops, portable hard drives, floppies, data cards, CDs, DVDs, mobile phones, PDAs, MP3 players, digital cameras and videos, and even Blackberries.
- Passwords: Must be kept strictly private and should be changed regularly.
- Clear the computer screen before the next patient comes into your consultation room.
- Dispose of printouts properly by shredding or incineration.
- Avoid allowing anything with personal data to be easily accessible to strangers.

- Do not install unfamiliar software in a computer system containing personal data.
- Log off after use.
- Keep the computer software up to date as to security patches and have anti-virus and anti-spyware programs with the appropriate firewall setting to protect the system.

The slogan that 'Everyone is responsible for Information Security' might have arisen from within the Hospital Authority. There is, however, no reason why this message should not apply to all members of the profession.

References and Further Reading

1. Personal Data (Privacy) Ordinance, Chapter 486 of the Laws of Hong Kong.

61

Duty of confidentiality

There are two aspects in which this duty could be examined.

The medical practitioner enjoys special rights to learn about matters of patients which are in the realm of the private, personal sphere. This privilege arises out of necessity as a result of the doctor-patient relationship to enable accurate diagnosis and appropriate treatment. It is also a reflection of the trust and confidence inherent in the relationship due to its very nature. A psychiatrist may come to know about a patient's secretive life. A physician might get to know about sensitive past medical history.

It is widely understood even to junior doctors that there is a duty to keep secrets and sensitive matter **strictly confidential**. Perhaps it is also helpful to be reminded that 'confidential' means to everyone, including even one's spouse and close friends.

A situation where one has no intention of revealing information but does so inadvertently is during casual conversations in public places, such as inside lifts or washrooms. It is thus not only good **etiquette and manners** always to be disciplined but also a matter of ethical practice.

Other '**risky areas**' include re-using paper with confidential information on the back, a computer 'logged-in' being left unattended, downloading data in unprotected USB drives and taking hospital records outside the hospital confines.

The legal basis of the duty of confidentiality is originally derived from the common law, largely as a result of ethical principles. It has now been supplemented by the Personal Data (Privacy) Ordinance, which prohibits the use of information for any purpose other than that at the time of collection and therefore communication to a third party.

Quite obviously, the duty outlasts the period of medical consultation and care. Does the duty end with the passing away of the patient? No. It is unethical to release confidential information derived from trust even upon the death of a patient. The obligation indeed should last forever.

Having said this, it must, however, be recalled that the duty is **not absolute** in the sense that disclosure may sometimes be required by law or in the public interest. Even in such circumstances, nevertheless, disclosure should be kept to the minimum required for its purpose.

The second perspective is when a doctor is an employee in a large institution. In this context, there is a general common law duty for an employee to uphold the secrets of the institution at which he works and information he acquires or comes to learn about in the course of his employment. This duty is called **fidelity** and is an implied term in the employment contract enforceable against both former and current employees. In addition, there may also be express confidentiality and restraint clauses limiting the time period after leaving the institution before such secrets could be released. Such restrictions are usually more commonly envisaged up the ladder of seniority. An employer in turn has a duty to notify his staff of the confidential nature of information or documents. In general, once information is in the public domain, it is unprotected under this rule. Examples of information falling within this category would be the contact addresses of the clientele of a private hospital or its business strategies in the coming years.

Violation of the common law duty just mentioned can be a justification for summary dismissal and may even constitute grounds for damages.

References and Further Reading
1. Personal Data (Privacy) Ordinance, Chapter 486 of the Laws of Hong Kong.
2. *Confidentiality: Protecting and Providing Information*. General Medical Council 2004 at GMC website under the List of Ethical Guidance at http://www.gmc-uk.org/guidance/ethical_guidance/index.asp.

3. *Confidentiality FAQs*. General Medical Council 2004 at GMC website under the List of Ethical Guidance at http://www.gmc-uk.org/guidance/current/library/confidentiality_faq.asp.

62

Medical records – 'Hospital Property: Patients Not Allowed to Read'!

It was once a common practice for the ward staff to put in big letters on the front of patients' folders the above 'warning' message. Is such a warning correct in the eyes of the law?

Basically the folder is indeed hospital property. It follows that you cannot read what is in my 'diary' without my permission. That sounds perfectly rational.

However, it is not to be forgotten that the information inside contains '**data**' relating to an individual. It is collected, recorded and then filed and stored in a retrievable manner, identifiable and accessible in relation to the person concerned, who is alive. It is therefore personal data subject to the Personal Data (Privacy) Ordinance, Chapter 486 of the Laws of Hong Kong.

Part V of the Ordinance governs **data access requests**. The patient, as the data subject, is entitled to request a copy of the information kept, under section 18. The hospital, as a **data user**, has to comply with a data access request not later than 40 days after receiving the request, under section 19.

The conclusion is therefore that if a patient wants to see what is in the notes, he has a right to request a copy of the notes from the hospital's Records Department.

The ward staff may wish to let the patient know the procedures to do so.

The **time limit** provided by the law also explains why doctors who are writing medical reports should ensure their readiness before it is too late. This time limit is usually within 40 days, section 19(1).

Is it always the case that patients, as a result of the foregoing, can demand access to their hospital records? The answer is no. For the medical practitioner, the relevant exemption to section 18 is found under section 59. Section 59 of the Personal Data (Privacy) Ordinance, enacted in 1995, stipulates that personal data relating to the physical or mental health of the data subject are exempt from the provisions of data protection principle 6 (which deals with access), and section 18(1)(b) (dealing with supply of a copy of held data), in any case in which the application of those provisions to the data would be 'likely to cause serious harm to the physical or mental health of either the data subject or any other individual'.

It is interesting to note that in England the same issue is governed by the Data Protection (Subject Access Modification) (Health) Order 2000 (No. 413). Section 5(1) of the Order states that personal data are exempt from section 7 (of the (English) Data Protection Act 1998) in any case to the extent to which the application of that section would be likely to cause serious harm to the physical or mental health or condition of the data subject or any other person. The wording of the provisions, like much among English and Hong Kong statutes, is thus essentially identical.

Finally, is the warning 'Medical Records – "Hospital Property: Patients Not Allowed to Read"' entirely wrong? Not quite. If it reads 'Medical Records – "Hospital Property: Not Allowed to Read"' without the word 'patients', then it is correct because it serves to warn away unrelated third parties from looking at the contents and that is what the professional should always be doing.

References and Further Reading
1. Personal Data (Privacy) Ordinance, Chapter 496 of the Laws of Hong Kong.
2. The Data Protection (Subject Access Modification) Health Order 2003 SI 19/03.
3. *Confidentiality: Protecting and Providing Information.* General Medical Council 2004 at GMC website under List of Ethical Guidance at http://www.gmc-uk.org/guidance/current/library/confidentiality.asp.

---
63 ---

Explaining a patient's condition to the relatives

It might appear at first sight obvious and straightforward that relatives are to be informed and kept updated of a patient's condition. That is very often done by many doctors.

Have we ever asked the question whether this practice is right?

The majority of doctors as well as patients or their relatives undoubtedly don't have a legal background and so the issue of talking to relatives about a patient's medical condition is not often considered at all. Properly speaking, however, a medical practitioner should obtain the **patient's consent** before the medical details of a patient are disclosed, even to the relatives. This includes even the spouse, parents, siblings, children, etc. This is a part of the duty of confidentiality.

An example will be convincing. A husband who contracted, say, gonorrhoea would be fully entitled to have that diagnosis kept secret from his spouse or partner, and the attending doctor would have no right to disclose anything unless with the husband's consent. The doctor would be liable for any consequence or damage arising as a result of such disclosure without consent from the husband.

It is therefore suggested that consent from the patient is to be obtained before any such communication to the relatives. For the same reason, if the patient does not want the relatives to know his condition, his wish prevails and the doctor should not yield even to demanding relatives.

That is the **legal position**. However, although the legal position is always high in importance and weighty in the evaluation of what step to take, it is not the only consideration. Here we are dealing with people and we are talking about **good medical practice**. The better way out is therefore to seek patients' consent to talk to their relatives early on, so that when it comes to the necessary moment, the cooperation of the relatives can be summoned by their recruitment into the management of the patient.

Having said this, it may be interesting to reflect upon a special case, the hypothetical, but yet arguably real, situation of the spouse or sexual partner of a patient who is confirmed as HIV-positive. Should the managing doctor of the HIV-positive patient inform the spouse or partner of the HIV status to protect him or her? A dilemma exists here owing to the conflict between the duties of confidentiality and that of protecting the innocent partner in the public interest. The partner would theoretically be in the category of the 'need to know'.

This has indeed not been an easy question to answer. A Guidance released by the General Medical Council in 2004 'Disclosures to Protect the Patient or Others' explained that disclosure of personal information without consent may be justified in the public interest where failure to do so may expose the patient or others to risk of death or serious harm. Consent is still vital unless the patient or others are exposed to a risk so serious that it outweighs the patient's privacy interest.

The medical practitioner in such a situation therefore has to draw the right balance to decide what to do. In the author's opinion, it is reasonableness that the courts are looking for in their judgments and provided the necessary explanations, warnings, and procedural steps and documentations have all been made, a doctor should have no fear to do what is ethically correct. After all, passing on a fatal infection to a partner knowingly is a criminal offence. Had a doctor given such a warning to an HIV-infected patient and the latter still refused to give consent to pass on the information, the doctor should not be considered wrong in having done something to prevent a crime.

Section 59 of the Personal Data (Privacy) Ordinance exempts personal data relating to the physical or mental health of a data subject from data protection principle 3 (concerning the use of data), if these provisions would cause serious harm to the health of the data subject or any other individual. It is therefore arguable that the section extends to protect a doctor who informs the HIV patient's partner in the circumstances. Along the same vein, this section should also exempt liability for sharing individual data with colleagues for the purpose of follow-up action, e.g. in a suspected child or wife abuse case.

References and Further Reading

1. *Disclosures to Protect the Patient or Others.* General Medical Council (2004), para 27.
2. Personal Data (Privacy) Ordinance, Chapter 496 of the Laws of Hong Kong.
3. The (UK) Data Protection (Subject Access Modification) Health Order 2003 SI 19/03.
4. *Confidentiality: Protecting and Providing Information.* General Medical Council 2004 at GMC website under List of Ethical Guidance at http://www.gmc-uk.org/guidance/current/library/confidentiality.asp.
5. *Confidentiality FAQs.* General Medical Council 2004 at GMC website under the List of Ethical Guidance at http://www.gmc-uk.org/guidance/current/library/confidentiality_faq.asp.

64

The Personal Data (Privacy) Ordinance

The Personal Data (Privacy) Ordinance (Chapter 486 of the Laws of Hong Kong) is a very important piece of statute, the provisions of which have far reaching consequences to everyone and most institutions in society. It also has direct and indirect bearings on the daily practice of all medical practitioners.

The following account is a brief summary of the essential features of the statute highlighting the salient features which the medical practitioner should be aware of.

Section 4 states that a data user shall not do an act, or engage in a practice, that contravenes the data protection principles stipulated in Schedule 1.

Section 18 concerns data access requests. An individual, or a relevant person on his behalf, may make a request to be informed by a data user whether the data user holds personal data of the data subject, and if the data user holds such data, to be supplied with a copy of such.

Section 19 depicts that such compliance must either be within 40 days or in the form of a written notice explaining why such compliance cannot be met, provided that the request is made with supply of the prescribed information, section 20.

Section 22 provides for correction of the data if erroneous.

Section 26 requires data no longer required for the purposes of its collection to be erased.

Section 28 allows a fee to be imposed for making a data access request, provided that such is not excessive, section 28(3).

There are six Schedules to the Ordinance, of which only Schedule 1 has implications to the medical practitioner.

Schedule 1 sets out the data protection principles:

- Principle 1 concerns the purpose and manner of data collection. Data collection must be fair and for a relevant and necessary lawful purpose and must not be excessive. The data subject must be informed of his rights.
- Principle 2 concerns the accuracy and retention of personal data. Retention should not be longer than is necessary for the fulfilment of the purpose for collection.
- Principle 3 is related to the use of personal data, which should not be for any other purpose than that for which it is collected.
- Principle 4 provides for the security of personal data. Practicable steps must be taken to ensure protection against unauthorised or accidental access, processing and erasure.
- Principle 5 stipulates that information has to be generally available as to the data user's policies and practices in relation to personal data.
- Principle 6 is access to personal data and confers the right to a data subject to ascertain whether a data user holds his personal data, to request access within a reasonable time at a fee which is not excessive, and to make corrections. Such requests may be refused provided that reasons are given.

The fact that these principles are in statutory law means that a data subject has the right to seek redress through the court if his or her rights are infringed in respect to the provisions.

As an aside, the medical practitioner who is perceptive will be aware that the statute is very narrow in relation to the protection of personal privacy and is limited mainly to systematically collected, retrievable data.

A person feeling aggrieved by practices not in accordance with the stipulations of the Ordinance may file a complaint to the Privacy Commissioner. The Commissioner will liaise with the parties to reach a resolution through mediation if the case satisfies the requirements. In the event of a serious breach, formal investigation will be carried out and enforcement measures will be undertaken. It is an offence in law to contravene an enforcement notice and is punishable by a fine or imprisonment.

At the time of writing, the Constitutional and Mainland Affairs Bureau (CMBA) has just released the Consultation Document on Review of the Personal Data (Privacy) Ordinance for public review and opinion. This exercise aims at updating the Ordinance in order to provide a more adequate protection of personal privacy to the people of Hong Kong. The reader is urged to follow the changes for his information.

References and Further Reading
1. Website of the Privacy Commissioner for Personal Data at http://www.pcpd.org.hk.
2. The Personal Data (Privacy) Ordinance (Chapter 486 of the Laws of Hong Kong).
3. Consultation Document on Review of the Personal Data (Privacy) Ordinance on the Privacy Commissioner for Personal Data's website: http://www.pcpd.org.hk/english/review_ordinance/files/PCPD_submission_ReviewPDPO_e.pdf.

IV

Negligence and Liability

65

What constitutes medical negligence?

Medical negligence is a term so often heard that it is easy to think that the two always go together. Actually, negligence is not something unique to the medical profession.

Medical negligence means negligence in relation to medical care. It is simply a special case of **professional negligence**. The word 'professional' does not necessarily mean only the traditionally regarded professionals such as the clergyman, the doctor or the lawyer. Any person who professes special skill in his particular trade is a professional. The word is construed widely.

A defendant who falls short of the standard of competence expected of a person who professes in his particular skill is negligent.

A doctor will be concerned with what the claimant would need to prove in order to be successful in a medical **negligence claim**. These are the existence of a duty of care; breach of the standard of care owed; and that the breach had caused damage. Each of these steps will be considered in great detail by the legal representatives of the parties concerned in order to prove or refute the validity of a claim.

It is thus not so easy a task to prove that a doctor is negligent unless there is an overt and palpable breach of standard or duty. A prudent and conscientious medical practitioner should have no worry of such litigation against him. Certainly a mere complication per se, which so often raises a concern among many colleagues, is far from being an established negligence.

Nevertheless, it is always advisable to seek legal opinion in the first instance to prevent a good case from turning into a bad one.

References and Further Reading

1. Kenyon Mason, Alexander McCall Smith, and Graeme Laurie. *Law and Medical Ethics*, 6th edn. LexisNexis Butterworths 2002; Chapter 9, pp 271-308.

2. Catherine Elliott, Frances Quinn. *Contract Law*, 3rd edn. Longman 2001; Chapter 2, pp 14-119.

— 66 —

The Koo test

This is a test the courts in Hong Kong are using for deciding whether a doctor defendant is negligent. The origin of the test is the case of *Dr. Koo v The Medical Council of Hong Kong* 1988.

A medical practitioner was ordered by the Medical Council to be removed from the Register for 3 months on the grounds that he had been guilty of '**misconduct in a professional respect**'. The Hong Kong Court of Appeal was to decide if the Medical Council erred in making the judgment of what is 'misconduct in a professional respect'.

The charge on which the doctor was convicted was that he had failed to exercise effective personal supervision over a nurse he employed, contrary to section 14 of the Warning Notice of the Hong Kong Medical Council 'Covering Improper Delegation of Medical Duties to Unregistered Persons'. The relevant portion reads:

'… the proper employment of nurses, midwives and other persons trained to perform specialized functions relevant or supplementary to medicine is entirely acceptable provided the medical practitioner concerned exercises **effective personal supervision** over any persons so employed… '

It was remarked by the court that the choice of the word 'effective' indicated that the Council intended to place a heavy responsibility upon doctors in this respect.

The evidence was that on 28 November 1986 a police constable in plain clothes visited the doctor's clinic asking for 10 tablets of Physeptone. The nurse, unable to find a registration card in the name of the constable, filled up a new card, wrote a prescription herself and sold the tablets from an unlocked drawer to the constable for $60.

The doctor's contention was that one particular incident was not in itself sufficient proof of lack of supervision.

In arriving at its decision, the court cited the English case of *Doughty v General Dental Council* (1987), an appeal by a dentist against a finding by the Professional Conduct Committee of the General Dental Council of 'serious professional misconduct'. In that judgment, Lord Mackay said, '… what is now required is that the General Dental Council should establish conduct connected with his profession in which the dentist concerned has fallen short, by omission or commission, of the standards of conduct expected among dentists and that such falling short as is established should be serious'. It was observed, however, that the Hong Kong ordinance does not require the element of seriousness, the relevant words being 'misconduct in *any* professional respect'.

The test is thus simply whether the doctor's conduct has **fallen short of the standard expected** among doctors.

The lesson is that a shortfall is a shortfall whether serious or not. Seriousness perhaps would only be of significance in the **sentencing** stage.

References and Further Reading

1. *Dr. Koo v The Medical Council of Hong Kong* (1988) HKCA 278; CACV000023/1988.
2. *Doughty v General Dental Council* (1987) AC 164.

67

Vicarious liability

What does this term mean? Why do doctors need to know about the term?

No exaggeration. If you ask anyone in hospital management or colleagues involved with risk management issues such as those in the patient relations department, you will be surprised as to why everyone knows the term so well. Of course, the reader who is less restricted in his general knowledge might also have come across the term.

Briefly, vicarious liability refers to the liability owed by an employer to a claim arising as a result of his employee's negligence or otherwise at work. In other words, the liability was originally due to the employee's fault and, because it was incurred in the course of employment, the employer becomes jointly and severally liable to the claimant. '**Jointly**' is easily understood from its plain English meaning. '**Severally**' means that the claimant can actually make his claim against either of or both defendants, and he will be able to claim the total of his awarded damages from either even though the total of his claims can only be up to the amount of the awarded damages.

A hospital is therefore very concerned with the liabilities incurred by its employees. Awards for claims against doctors' negligence are obviously of great amounts and therefore the hospital is often sued instead or additionally as a joint defendant.

This is exactly the reason why a modern hospital should be diligent in its **risk management** measures. A very major expenditure item in the budget account is payroll. No less, however, are payments in settlement and damages unless risks are well managed.

References and Further Reading

1. Catherine Elliott, Frances Quinn. *Contract Law*, 3rd edn. Longman 2001; Chapter 13, pp 277-286.

68

What besides simple negligence?

Every modern-day doctor is familiar to varying degrees with the issue of negligence. To recapitulate, negligence in a professional sense means breach of the standard duty of care expected for a reasonable average person in the trade, i.e. the practice of medicine. To be a claimable negligence, the plaintiff will also need to prove the **existence of a duty** in the first place, the **breach**, **damage** and a **causal relationship** between the breach and the damage suffered. In essence, one can roughly take it that the layman's understanding is that simple negligence is carelessness.

This is perhaps all what most knowledgeable medical practitioners know about 'medical negligence'. In reality, however, there is another variety which is less often encountered and therefore not so well known.

Gross negligence or the equivalent, criminal negligence, refers to an act which amounts in its seriousness to a crime. The test for gross negligence was laid down in the landmark case of *R v Bateman* (1925). The court said: '… the facts must be such that, in the opinion of the jury, the negligence of the accused went beyond a mere matter of compensation between subjects and showed such disregard for the life and safety of others as to amount to a crime against the State and conduct deserving punishment'.

It is perhaps helpful to the reader for his better understanding of the concept to cite the famous case of *R v Adomako* (1995). An anaesthetist failed to notice that the endotracheal tube had become disconnected because he went across to an adjacent operating room to attend a concomitant surgery. The patient died and the anaesthetist was prosecuted for manslaughter from gross negligence. On appeal to the House of Lords, the conviction was upheld.

In other words, whether a negligent act is simple or gross is dependent upon its severity, i.e. how bad it is in the circumstances of the case, as judged by the reasonable man.

A simple negligence gives rise to a civil claim; a gross negligent act (or omission where a duty of care is owed) opens one up to a criminal prosecution.

References and Further Reading

1. Smith John. *Smith & Hogan Criminal Law*, 9th edn. Butterworths 1999; Chapter 5, pp 90-96.
2. Kenyon Mason, Alexander McCall Smith, and Graeme Laurie. *Law and Medical Ethics*, 6th edn. LexisNexis Butterworths 2002; Chapter 9, pp 305-308.
3. *R v Bateman* (1925) 19 Cr App Rep 335.
4. *R v Adomako* (1995) 1 AC 171.

69

To seek legal advice
– is it necessary or advisable?

Doctors are highly educated intellectuals and are often proud of their achievements. This is what they rightly deserve. No doubt about that. The author's personal experience with his colleagues and doctor friends therefore tells him that doctors are quite frequently of the view that, should there be a need for them to appear in court as a result of being sued, they are themselves the most able persons to explain and defend their case. Many would even think that they do not need to speak through the mouth of a lawyer.

There is, however, only some truth in this belief and the belief is actually very dangerous. It is correct that the concerned doctors know the details of the case best. The court would have no query about this and that is why such doctors have to provide the relevant facts and be cross-examined.

However, it must be realised that what is to happen in the court is not a rehearsed **mortality and morbidity census** discussion. The judge, the lawyers and the jury, if present, are, in any event, not equipped for that. What is going to take place is in reality a presentation of arguments from both sides on the merits of their case. The English (and therefore Hong Kong under the Basic Law) legal system is adversarial, meaning that the parties are to 'fight' in the courtroom with the judge and the jury members watching and deciding who should win. The court would be assimilating the factual evidence to test whether certain legal points could be established. 'Applying the law to the facts' is the key step which is often stressed to law students.

An appropriate example here is whether a particular damage is causally related to an alleged negligent act or omission. The court would in this case be interested in whether, for example, the 'but for' test is satisfied, i.e. but for the negligence, the damage would not have been suffered. However, this is not the only test and any further elaboration will start to confuse. The 'layman' medical practitioner will then encounter difficulties over what to highlight to establish or refute legal points which may lead to certain conclusions. This is just one example and there may be many legal points to be established. Each point might involve lengthy arguments and citing of legal precedents and discussions of legal principles from both parties.

The end result is that, far from a discussion of medical facts and opinion, the court is concerned with **a legal battle**. It is an intense argument of legal principles, case law, statutes, customs, and their interpretation and application.

It should now be clear that it is very silly to appear unrepresented. Even if one is an expert in a particular medical field and is highly competent, that expertise is of not much relevance in the courtroom arguments. Indeed, the medical expert would be a total layman to the procedures and legal knowledge which are required to comprehend and follow what is happening. This is in the territory of the legal expert and there should be no logical reason to disadvantage oneself by choosing to be handicapped.

What you regard as important and crucial medical findings and facts may be totally irrelevant in a legal sense. What you see as unimportant could be essential in establishing a legal point.

Do not regret it when it is too late!

70

No admission

Doctors are mostly good natured and are kind and honest at heart. This is no surprise in view of their voluntary choice in taking up the profession and from their upbringing.

When things unfortunately turn out to be wrong or unexpected, doctors will have a tendency or urge to assume responsibility. There is nothing wrong with this. However, it is paramount to remember that one should never admit that there is wrong or fault on any party in making a humble response. This does not mean telling lies but it should be emphasised that whether someone is liable or not is judged in the eyes of the law, an area in which the 'layman' medical practitioner is usually ignorant or at the best an outsider. With **liability** having to be established at pains by the claimant, what sense does it make therefore to voluntarily admit it yourself? To have admitted liability is to make it less likely that your lawyer can help with your defence. It also means that you have cooperated with the claimant to incriminate yourself. With that piece of advice a sensible doctor should know better what to do should this occurrence arise.

Another significance of self-confession is with the **professional insurance** scheme. It is important to note carefully the terms of one's insurance or indemnity plan and whether self-admission or settlement before the insurer is informed would void the policy altogether. This would be disastrous as it could mean that the medical protection fees subscribed would all be wasted, leaving one without the 'protection'. Moreover, the heavy compensation one would have to pay would end up not recoverable!

It is critically important, however, that the above is not confused with the immensely relevant policy of maintenance of a good-doctor relationship with the patient in the event of a medical error having been made. The well publicised world-wide trend in open disclosure in candid, truthful and honest terms of factual details is welcomed by patients and is essential in preserving the trust and confidence necessary to good compliance with the required additional medical treatment resulting from the error and in reducing the litigation risk of the particular doctor.

References and Further Reading

1. Hodgin Ray. *Insurance Law: Text and Materials*, 2nd edn. Routledge-Cavendish 2002; Chapter 3 Making and breaking the insurance contract, pp 121-134.
2. Birds John, Hird Norma. *Bird's Modern Insurance Law*, 6th edn. Sweet & Maxwell 2004; Chapter 7 Warranties and conditions, pp 142-166.

71

Causation of damage – proven?

Causation is an interesting issue in the law and it is both necessary and interesting for the doctor to understand a little more of this topic.

Let us start with an example. X injured Y by hitting him. X would not have hit Y had Y not been drinking and become out of control. However, Y had hit X first because X took Y's pocket money the month before. Y, on the other hand, would not have been so angry had he not been scolded bitterly by his mother that morning for his failure in his school test. Y failed the test because X maliciously replaced old batteries in Y's calculator so that it malfunctioned and Y subsequently found this out. X did that because Y had teased X earlier for X's poor achievements in mathematics. Y did that because X had laughed at Y for Y's poor performance in physical training. X…

Which cause is **the cause**? How do we decide which cause to take as the cause?

This is important in the medical context. Suppose a robber stabbed a young woman in the abdomen with a sharp knife. The woman bled heavily and was in shock when she reached hospital. She was resuscitated and given a blood transfusion. Then she was diagnosed with a lacerated spleen requiring emergency splenectomy. What would be the cause of her death if:

- There was a mismatched transfusion; or,
- The surgeon had by mistake left a bleeder untied at operation; or,
- The anaesthetist had given a wrong dose of medication; or,
- There was an undiagnosed pneumothorax?

What if there was a combination of the above? Can the doctor who committed an error claim that the patient would not have been subject to his mistake but for the robber's crime, and thus attribute the cause of the patient's death to the robbery?

There is enough confusion and it is time to clarify.

When there is a single direct immediate cause, the usual test the courts use is the '**but for**' test. This means that if the damage would not have occurred or been suffered but for the act or omission of the defendant, it is caused by that conduct of the defendant.

When there is more than one cause or there is a series of causes, different approaches have been taken by the courts.

It may be that all the causes are considered material and a relative weight is given to each, with the respective defendants then to be responsible for their individual contribution to the damage.

Alternatively, when the causes are serial in nature, the court may examine if there is a break in the **chain of causation**, such that there is an independent act in a particular step which cannot be said to be linked to the previous step. An example would be a D knocking out P leaving P unconscious on a street corner, and P's head being hit by a falling heavy bottle thrown from a window in the building above so that as a result P subsequently died.

It is important to realise that negligence claims, about which doctors are particularly worried, require **proof of causation** on the part of the claimant. With a better idea of causation issues in mind, perhaps we will be a little wiser when next time we sense a potential cause for concern. It is, however, always better and preferable to call one's legal advisor in view of the complexity of the law.

The issue is interesting and a number of real medico-legal cases will be instructive.

In *Barnett v Chelsea and Kensington Hospital Management Committee* (1968), a watchman arrived in casualty early one morning nauseated after a cup of tea. The casualty doctor simply advised that he should consult his GP. The man died 5 hours later of arsenic poisoning. Action for negligence failed because there was evidence that even if he had been examined it was too late for any treatment to save him. It was not a case of but for the hospital's negligence he would not have died.

In *Brooks v Home Office* (1999), a woman prisoner had been pregnant with twins, one of which had died. Despite the fact that on ultrasound scan one of the twins appeared not to be developing properly, the prison doctor observed the woman for 5 days before referring her for specialist advice. The affected twin had died 2 days after the scan. Ms. Brooks sued, arguing that the standard of health care was below that outside prison. The court, however, found that a wait of 2 days was reasonable. As the baby died within this time the doctor's negligence had not caused its death.

A multiple causes situation was seen in *McGhee v National Coal Board* (1972), where Mr. McGhee had developed dermatitis to brick dust at work. This risk could have been lessened if showers had been installed. The latter was therefore just an additional cause to Mr. McGhee's own allergy. The House of Lords decided that where the negligence was a substantial contribution to the injury the employer could be liable and negligence need not be the sole cause.

In *Wilsher v Essex Area Health Authority* (1988), a premature baby was twice given too much oxygen and as a result, it was claimed, suffered from permanent blindness. However, medical evidence suggested that the baby's blindness could also have been caused by several other medical conditions from which he suffered. On a balance of probabilities, therefore, it was not known if the doctor's breach was the material cause of the injury as it was merely another possible cause.

In *Hotson v East Berkshire Health Authority* (1987), a young boy fell, injuring his knee, and developed complications. Initial X-ray missed a femoral neck fracture, which was picked up only 5 days later. Avascular necrosis developed. Medical evidence then showed that there was a 25 per cent chance of the complication even if the diagnosis had been made on the first visit. The House ruled against the boy because the standard of proof required, i.e. on a balance of probabilities, means proving that it was more likely that the negligence had caused the damage than that it had not, i.e. at least a 51 per cent chance.

A breakage in the chain of causation occurred in *Thompson v Blake James* (1998). A doctor was sued by the parents of a child with measles complicated by meningitis resulting in brain damage. He had advised against immunisation when the child was 6 months old because of the child's medical history. However, the decision not to immunise her was not taken until a year later, after the parents had consulted other doctors. The advice from the other doctors was held an intervening event which broke the chain of causation. The parents were not relying on the defendant's advice.

A further example illustrates that the damage has to be the relevant damage. In *Brown v Lewisham and North Southwark Health Authority* (1999), the plaintiff was discharged from hospital A after a coronary bypass surgery during which heparin had been given. It transpired that he developed a deep vein thrombosis on the way back to the original referring hospital B. For that reason heparin was restarted but he developed heparin-induced thrombocytopenia, a sensitivity reaction, with worsening of the thrombosis, eventually necessitating a mid-thigh amputation of his left leg. His contention that the negligence in the early discharge from hospital A was responsible for his damage failed in the (English) Court of Appeal. That was not the cause of his damage because the doctors in hospital A could not have foreseen the thrombosis or the sensitivity reaction and so they were not liable.

The reader may have noticed that it is very difficult to follow the cases with a clear line of consistency. This is exactly why the law is complicated as each case depends upon its specific facts. It is important to remember to pay your defence union bills.

No treatise on this subject would be sufficient if the recent development in the House of Lords decision in *Chester v Afshar* (2004) was not mentioned. This is a very interesting case which deserves a slightly more detailed description and analysis in order to understand its potential significance.

In *Chester v Afshar* (2004), a consultant neurosurgeon operated on a lady with low back pain without giving prior warning of the risk of postoperative paralysis. The patient indeed suffered from the complication but the doctor was not found to be negligent in the operation. Nevertheless, the patient was successful in her claim of damage. The House rejected the neurosurgeon's appeal by 3:2. The gist of the argument was that the need for patients to receive sufficient information from medical professionals is so great that a patient who can show that he or she might have done something else or taken an alternative course should be able to claim damages. In other words, even if a patient was unable to prove damage as a result of negligent surgery, he or she would be entitled to compensation if it was proven that with the appropriate information he or she would have sought another better expert or refused surgery, etc. This is therefore a slight but important development from the traditional model of causation based on policy considerations. It represents a new potential line of attack on the profession and warrants particular attention from all practitioners.

References and Further Reading

1. Catherine Elliott, Frances Quinn. *Contract Law*, 3rd edn. Longman 2001; pp 92-106.
2. *Barnett v Chelsea and Kensington Hospital Management Committee* (1968) 1 QB 428.
3. *Brooks v Home Office* (1999) 2 FLR 33.
4. *McGhee v National Coal Board* (1972) 3 All ER 1008.
5. *Wilsher v Essex Area Health Authority* (1988) AC 1074.
6. *Hotson v East Berkshire Health Authority* (1987) AC 750.
7. *Thompson v Blake James* (1998) Lloyd's Rep Med 187.
8. *Brown v Lewisham and North Southwark Health Authority* (1999) Lloyd's Rep Med 110.
9. *Chester v Afshar* (2004) UKHL 41.

Relevance of the Limitation Ordinance

There is a **time limit** by which a claim must be initiated or the liability will expire. The time limits for different claims are different and are dictated and found in the Limitation Ordinance, Chapter 347 of the Laws of Hong Kong. The most relevant for the medical practitioner is section 27 which governs personal injuries actions for damages for negligence, nuisance or breach of duty. '**Personal injuries**' include any disease and any impairment of a person's physical or mental condition, subsection 2.

Subsection 3 stipulates that such actions are not to be brought after the expiration of the period specified in subsections (4) and (5).

According to subsection (4), the period is 3 years from:

(a) the date on which the cause of action accrued; or

(b) the date (if later) of the claimant's knowledge.

According to subsection (5), if the person injured dies before the expiration of the period in subsection (4), the period in respect of the cause of action surviving for the benefit of the estate of the deceased is 3 years from:

(a) the date of death; or

(b) the date of the personal representative's knowledge, whichever is later.

A person's **date of knowledge** refers to that on which he first had knowledge, subsection 6:

(a) that the injury was significant; and

(b) that it was attributable to the act or omission alleged; and

(c) of the identity of the defendant.

If therefore a personal injuries claim is not brought within the time limit of 3 years subject to the qualifications above, the cause of action expires technically, forthwith, without more and automatically.

A practitioner who has been worrying may then have his fears allayed although in exceptional circumstances the court may exercise its equitable discretion to override the limit, section 30. It must also be noted that the limit applies only to the initiation of action not its completion. Furthermore, if the cause of action is in negligence not personal injury, the limit will default to the general time limit of 6 years for tort actions.

A further point to note is the effect of section 22, which covers the claimant with a disability. That includes one who is an **infant** in law (otherwise referred to as a 'minor'), meaning being less than 18 years of age (section 2 of the Age of Majority (Related Provisions) Ordinance). Subsection 2 of section 22 provides for a period of 3 years after the reaching of 18 years during which action may be taken if the claimant was an infant when the right of action accrued.

References and Further Reading

1. Limitation Ordinance, Chapter 347 of the Laws of Hong Kong.
2. Age of Majority (Related Provisions) Ordinance, Chapter 410 of the Laws of Hong Kong.

73

The real significance of legal costs

Why is it that we do not want to be involved in litigations? Maybe it is entrenched tradition. Maybe we do not understand much of the law as a layman to that field. Maybe we have better things to do. But a very real worry is often legal cost.

Legal cost means the money expenditure involved in litigation in relation to legal advice, investigation, preparation and representation. This is in turn divisible into **retainer** fees and expenses, and **disbursements**, and an estimate with costs on account is usually payable in advance. Besides the final bill, interim bills may also be issued in a prolonged dispute process. A client is entitled to a bill with full breakdown of items of costs. These are common sense.

What is more often overlooked is the significance on legal costs in terms of the risks for a litigant.

First, a verdict is separately given to the decision on legal costs. Very often the winning party will also get legal costs but this is not a must. An indulgent party asking for an extension of time, for example, being unable to be prepared on time for an interim application, may eventually be penalised on costs despite winning the case overall. The **order on costs** is usually given by the judge after the verdict. To get one's costs means that the other party is to pay for your legal costs. However, the possibility of being liable for the opposite party's legal fees can be a deterrent to the initiation of an action.

Second, where a **claimant is impecunious**, he is entitled to legal aid. Doctors, on the other hand, are invariably too well off to pass the means test to qualify for such benefit. Costs are usually not paid by the impecunious claimant supported by the Legal Aid Department but by the Director of Legal Aid. A poor man is thus advantaged in that he would be free from the liability to pay costs even if he loses his case. The doctor, on the other hand, is fully liable for costs if he loses. Having said that, a claimant seeking legal aid has to pass a merits test as well and will not be able to receive assistance if he cannot show reasonable grounds for taking action.

References and Further Reading

1. Patrick Chan (editor-in-chief). *Hong Kong Civil Procedure 2009.* Volume 1. Order 62. Sweet & Maxwell.
2. Wilkinson Michael, Booth Christine, Cheung Eric. *The Student Guide to Civil Procedure in Hong Kong*, 2nd edn. LexisNexis 2005; Chapter 20, pp 812-854.
3. Bokhary (editor). *Archbold Criminal Law Pleading, Evidence & Practice 2009*. Sweet & Maxwell; Chapter 6 Costs and legal aid in criminal proceedings.

The Court and Attendance

───── 74 ─────

Court summons as a witness

A medical practitioner may be summoned to attend the court for various reasons.

The most common reason is to provide **evidence of fact**. This is the case of an Accident and Emergency Department doctor attending court to describe the nature of an injury or a doctor from an Orthopaedics Department to inform the court of the recovery during follow-up. A doctor may be summoned if he is a material witness for either the prosecution or the accused in a criminal prosecution, or as a witness in a civil litigation such as to describe in a probate dispute the mental capacity of a deceased person when making a will at the terminal stage.

A less common reason is that of more senior doctors attending as **expert witnesses**. They are there to assist the court in medical matters which the court needs to know in order to make a decision. Doctors in this category are usually reputed members of the profession or holders of important positions in the public service.

A doctor may of course be involved in the capacity of an ordinary citizen unrelated to being a doctor, whether he or she is expected to be able to provide evidence of facts or be actually a litigant.

A doctor, however, would NOT be asked to attend court as a member of **the jury**. This is an exception following similar long-time practice in English law.

In fact, exception from the duty to serve as a jury member includes several other categories of people as well. The first category consists of those 'deemed to be ineligible' on the basis of their employment or vocation, such as judges, justices of the peace, the legal profession, the police and probation officers, and the clergy. People 'disqualified to serve' comprise the second group and are those who have been sentenced to a term of imprisonment, with a criminal record or on bail in criminal proceedings. The medical profession is included under the third category of 'excused as of right' together with the armed forces. A full listing of the exempted categories of people can be found under section 5 of the Jury Ordinance, Chapter 3 of the Laws of Hong Kong.

An interesting incident the author happened to have come across is this. A respectful and conscientious hospital resident came to the Division Head's office holding a court summons in her hand and asked to be released on the following day for **court attendance** in a case of AOABH, i.e. assault occasioning actual bodily harm. The boss, probably suffering from a hard time with insufficient staff, said sternly, 'Tell my secretary to call them up to say that you are too busy to attend.' This is, the author must say, very embarrassing. Failure to attend court in response to a summons can potentially amount to contempt of the court in the absence of good justification. The law is stated in section 36 of the Criminal Procedure Ordinance, Chapter 221 of the Laws of Hong Kong. Disobeying a witness order or summons to attend court without just excuse is punishable summarily as contempt and is liable to imprisonment not exceeding 2 years.

Whether you like to go to court or not, the message is clear: You need to attend when you are wanted.

References and Further Reading
1. Jury Ordinance, Chapter 3 of the Laws of Hong Kong.
2. Criminal Procedure Ordinance, Chapter 221 of the Laws of Hong Kong.

75

Court attendance – are you an expert?

Young doctors are often involved in a **court summons**. This is because they are usually the first front-line person in charge of patients coming either to the Accident and Emergency or when patients are admitted into a hospital.

When a doctor is summoned to the court to give evidence of facts, they are in the strict sense not experts but ordinary **fact witnesses**. They are no different in this scenario from the man on the street who saw what happened. They are standing in the witness box merely to help the court to understand the facts in relation to the circumstances of a case and to enable the establishment of some factual conclusion. A doctor in such a situation would be required to provide usually the findings of his physical examination or treatment.

Who and when then is a doctor **an expert** in the court? This is when you are there to give opinion and knowledge on points of medicine which the court needs but does not possess to assist it to understand the case. Such opinion is usually important in helping the court to reach a conclusion on a specific aspect of the case in question. Usually the expert would have been asked to write a report earlier in the course of the litigation and he should have done some preparation in the form of research on the topic. He is usually picked because he is a known authority in the field and has accepted an earlier request to take up the position. The expert is therefore often a very senior member of the profession. He performs this duty of his own free will and is often highly paid for his contribution.

There are a few criteria which help in deciding if one is an expert in a particular situation:

- Is one an authority in the respective field?
- Has one produced any relevant scientific publications on the subject?
- Has one been on the committees of international conferences and meetings in the particular area?
- Has one a professorship with any major university?
- How senior is one in the field?
- Has one been on the Board of the relevant professional accrediting body?
- Has one been on the committees of relevant professional societies?
- How highly regarded is one in the field?
- How senior was one in the hierarchy of the hospital before entering private practice?

In the past, parties often chose their own experts and differences in opinions between experts could and did cause controversies and difficulties for the courts. Nowadays, the courts usually require parties to agree beforehand upon a single expert so as to avoid confusion.

In the majority of cases, therefore, a doctor appearing in court does so in the capacity of a fact witness. The message is thus clearly that one is to provide facts and no opinion or interpretation of facts should be made unless requested to do so.

References and Further Reading

1. *Expert Witness Guidance*. British Medical Association 2006 at www.b ma.org.uk/ap.nsf/Content/Expertwitness.
2. *Code of Guidance on Expert Evidence: A guide for experts and those instructing them for the purpose of court proceedings*. Clinical Risk 2002; 8: 60-66.
3. Kirsten Miller. *On experts and immunity*. Casebook. Medical Protection Society 2008; 16(3): 7.
4. Kirsten Miller. *How safe are expert witnesses?* Casebook. Medical Protection Society 2005; 13(2): 25-26.

76

Cross-examination vs examination

Doctors are well trained to perform examinations on patients. They are, however, not much trained, if at all, for cross-examination. Of course, doctors do not have to be able to cross-examine but it is preferable, at least, for them to understand what cross-examination is. This is because they might be subject to cross-examination at some time in their career and this is often, for the many who are caught unprepared, not only a difficult time but also an embarrassing experience.

What is meant by cross-examination? Cross-examination refers to the questioning process done by the opposite party's lawyer after the examination-in-chief of one's own witnesses in a court trial or similar tribunal or professional body hearings. It is a step in the court's procedure that aims at allowing elicitation of weaknesses in the opposite party's case by the legal representatives.

The English court system and procedure as practised in Hong Kong is **adversarial** in nature. Each party is allowed to present his case and query the opponent's so as to enable the judge or jury to reach its own conclusion. To damage your case, your opponent's lawyers will do their best to cast doubt on what you say and on your medical findings. Not uncommonly they will do it so skilfully that a doctor could feel humiliated. They will lead you to contradict yourself so that you appear either incredible or foolish. They may try to demonstrate with their legal ways that you are not a prudent person. Typically you are not allowed the chance to elaborate your answers nor given much time to think about your answers. Only very quick yes's and no's are prompted. Doctors are understandably unused to the process and could easily be pushed into corners from where there is no escape. The doctor is also not to forget that such is the day in, day out daily bread of lawyers attending the court and in particular barristers (called counsels) that it is no wonder they have such an unmatchable advantage.

So, next time you go to the courts, remember to review your case materials thoroughly and be always clear in your mind what to say, not the least for the reputation of the profession. Cross-examinations are often done by people who are cross, and they are also often meant to be done in a cross manner.

References and Further Reading

1. Mauet Thomas, McCrimmon Les. *Fundamentals of Trial Techniques*. Law Book Co of Australasia 2000.

77

Entitlement to fees for court attendance by a doctor

Doctors, particularly the more junior ones, are often required to write medical reports. Depending on the specialty in which one works, there can be at times quite a number lining up for completion before prescribed deadlines.

For a number of the medical reports written, a doctor may also be required in due course to attend the court in relation to the cases.

It is an often-asked question whether a doctor who has attended court should be entitled to receive the fees for attendance of court.

The answer here lies in the **capacity** in which one is attending the court.

If a doctor is attending in the capacity of an expert witness, a prior agreement should have been made with the party contracting for his services. The fee is thus from that party and not the court. In reality, if the party wins eventually, the court may subject the costs of the expert to taxation, i.e. cost estimation, and the actual award may be less if it is in the opinion of the taxing master that the expert and his service are worth less. This occurs when the winning party asks for its costs to be awarded by the court and the court agrees that that should be paid by the opposite party. If the party loses the case, the expert's cost will be paid by the losing party employing him.

In the more common situation of attendance as a fact witness, the doctor should be entitled to the usual fees for witnesses, subject to one exception. When the doctor is **under employment** and the attendance is a part of his work duties, he may not be entitled to receive the fee unless there is prior agreement by the employer. The reason for this is because the attendance is tantamount to work performed in the course of employment, meaning that the attendance is on behalf of the institution of employment. The employer is thus entitled not the doctor.

The same rationale holds when doctors are asked to write medical reports. Despite the additional burden, it is merely regarded as a part of normal work duties and the fee paid by the requesting party such as a law firm is always to the credit of the employing institution.

References and Further Reading

1. Patrick Chan (editor-in-chief). *Hong Kong Civil Procedure 2009*. Volume 1. Order 62. Sweet & Maxwell.
2. Wilkinson Michael, Booth Christine, Cheung Eric. *The Student Guide to Civil Procedure in Hong Kong*, 2nd edn. LexisNexis 2005; Chapter 20, pp 812-854.
3. Bokhary (editor). *Archbold Criminal Law Pleading, Evidence & Practice 2009*. Sweet & Maxwell; Chapter 6 Costs and legal aid in criminal proceedings.

78

Writing expert opinions – charging, competence and liability

When a medical practitioner picks up the phone to find that he/she is being asked to act as an expert in a court case, often the following issues will arise:

- Are you eligible to be an expert and to accept an offer of writing up an expert opinion?
- Are you free to charge as much as you wish so long as the party requesting the report agrees?
- Are you subject to liability for negligence as a result of writing an unsatisfactory report?

The requesting party might be a law firm, the police, or the Legal Aid Department, etc, and will usually briefly outline the case and seek your view as to whether you can take up the case.

First, who is **an expert**? Whether a particular doctor is an expert is for the judge to decide. Factors such as qualifications, training and experience are relevant in the consideration. The ultimate test is whether one possesses the necessary expertise so as to enable the formulation of the required opinion. Basically, the purpose of the court in asking for an expert opinion is to summon the necessary expertise required for it to determine an issue which falls outside its expertise. It is therefore clear that the expert's opinion is of an assisting nature only, and the final decisive opinion remains that of the judge or the jury. Indeed the court has the discretion to decide how much weight to give to the expert's opinion. In the first section of a professionally written expert opinion, it is customary for the expert to enumerate his qualifications and experience, such as his number of years in the field, his position in university service and the number of relevant publications he has produced.

Second, **charging**. It might seem obvious to the reader that the offer and acceptance of writing an expert opinion is a straight forward agreement between two parties and therefore, owing to the English concept of freedom of contract, no third party can intervene with the terms provided that the contract is not illegal. This is all nice and simple and is correct. However, should the case proceed all the way to court, which is actually uncommon because parties usually will have settled in due course, the court will decide upon the fees warranted according to the usefulness of the opinion in the case. The taxing master will estimate the amount of fees allowed depending on the complexity of the facts, the amount of time spent and the standing of the expert. There is therefore no guarantee that the commissioning party, even if he wins the case and is awarded the costs, can recover the exact amount of the fees paid to the expert.

Third, is it safe to be an expert witness? The traditional position is that it is. The rationale of **immunity from negligence** claims was originally developed to give individuals the confidence to give evidence at trial without fear of reprisal. However, this needs to be updated in view of recent changes. It is increasingly being argued that experts are professionals who are paid for their expertise and therefore should be subject to the same rules of negligence as professionals so that the injured party can seek redress for any loss incurred. The topic has become a rather hot one in recent years in the United Kingdom and already it is becoming clear that in civil litigations, only those reports prepared for the principal purpose of testifying in court would attract witness immunity. It is notable that the argument that the overriding duty of an expert is to the court rather than the party employing the expert is no longer considered a valid reason to support the long held 'blanket immunity' given to barristers since the famous case of *Arthur JS Hall & Co v Simon* (2002).

Most of the claims arising in this context allege negligent underestimation of prognosis causing an undervaluation in the amount of settlements. In the article 'How safe are expert witnesses?' by Kirsten Miller in volume 13 of Casebook published by the Medical Protection Society in 2005, the author advised against being pressed for particular conclusions and raised the importance of including further treatment as a suggestion when it is indicated. In any event, it is prudent not to express any opinion outside the scope of one's expertise.

The interested reader is referred to the Code of Guidance on Expert Evidence 2001, which was produced by a Working Party set up by the then Head of Civil Justice in England in relation to the Woolf civil reform and the implementation of the Civil Procedure Rules 1998.

References and Further Reading

1. *Expert Witness Guidance*. British Medical Association 2006 at www.bma.org.uk/ap.nsf/Content/Expertwitness.
2. *Code of Guidance on Expert Evidence: A guide for experts and those instructing them for the purpose of court proceedings*. Clinical Risk 2002; 8: 60-66.
3. Kirsten Miller. *On experts and immunity*. Casebook. Medical Protection Society 2008; 16(3): 7.
4. Kirsten Miller. *How safe are expert witnesses?* Casebook. Medical Protection Society 2005; 13(2): 25-26.
5. *Acting as an Expert Witness* 2008. General Medical Council at GMC website under the List of Ethical Guidance at http://www.gmc-uk.org/guidance/ethical_guidance/expert_witness_guidance.asp.

79

Without prejudice and legal professional privilege

A close colleague of the author once jokingly offered to pay the author one dollar to read a letter the colleague was about to send out, which, according to him, was to be 'without prejudice'. His assumption was that that act would give the contents of his letter privilege by establishing a lawyer-client relationship between himself and the author.

Total mistake! Not only was the author not a registered practising solicitor, the court looks at the substance of things rather than mere procedures and, in any event, it is not a matter of whether a lawyer is involved but whether there was a genuine intention to settlement. Apparently, the concept was also confused with legal privilege.

Let us put things right.

A letter written with the big words '**without prejudice**' means that the details of facts disclosed in the content of that letter are not to be made public in any subsequent possible dispute litigation proceedings because those facts are there for the purpose of a settlement. The rationale for this rule is that the courts favour settlement instead of litigation as a way to resolve disputes so that the facts which may prejudice any particular party are given special status and need not be made open to the court. Having said this, it may remain for the court to decide if the words 'without prejudice' are effective or not, particularly if in the eyes of the court there was no genuine attempt at settlement.

'**Legal professional privilege**' means that confidential facts or documents released to a solicitor in a client's consultation for legal advice are privileged and thus cannot be required to be disclosed in court by the other parties. The privilege also extends to confidential facts or documents between the client or his legal advisor and third parties if their dominant purpose was for the preparation of a pending or anticipated litigation. The basis for such a rule lies in the respect for a fundamental right of a person to seek and consult legal advice privately and confidentially. A lawyer-client relationship is thus a pre-requisite in this situation.

The two concepts are entirely independent and separate. Simple though the above may seem, the reality is that there are many technical exceptions and points to be noted. Thus whether a particular piece of fact is privileged and inadmissible or warrants an injunction as to its discovery can itself be the issue of a preliminary part of a litigation, forming a mini-trial known as an interlocutory proceeding, within a big trial!

Indeed, this is a situation where the potential confusion illustrates vividly when and why the lawyer's assistance is indicated.

References and Further Reading

1. Wilkinson Michael, Booth Christine, Cheung Eric. *The Student Guide to Civil Procedure in Hong Kong*, 2nd edn. LexisNexis 2005; Chapter 20, pp 812-854.

80

Security for costs

This is an illustration of the complexities of the law and its procedures and serves as a warning to doctors not to overlook the importance of legal advice.

Litigants are often unaware of the significance of legal advice, preparation and representation. **Costs of legal service** are very often very high and, not uncommonly, can exceed the amount of compensation sought.

Security for costs means payment by order of the court as **security for anticipated costs** in legal proceedings when the court has reasonable grounds to believe that a litigant is unlikely to be able to pay the same if the eventual judgment is against him. The legal basis for this power is from Order 23 rule 1(1) of the Rules of the High Court of Hong Kong, as recorded in the Hong Kong Civil Procedure (the 'White Book').

In practice, such a decision by the court is usually made on a foreign claimant ordinarily residing outside the jurisdiction. The rationale behind this is that an **unmeritorious litigant** may merely be a man of straw.

The relevance in seeking an order from the court for security for costs is illustrated by a local case where a plastic surgeon was sued by an American client for facial scarring after laser resurfacing was performed on her. The client subsequently went back to the United States and sued the Hong Kong doctor. The strategy employed by the lawyers of the Hong Kong doctor was to seek such an order. If the court concurs with the application and the foreign litigant is not able to make such a payment, all proceedings will be stayed. Of course, the court must carry out a balancing exercise. On the one hand it must weigh the injustice to the plaintiff if prevented from pursuing a proper claim by an order for security. Against that, it must weigh the injustice to the defendant if no security is ordered and the defendant finds him or herself unable to recover costs from the plaintiff in due course.

To the author's knowledge, the case was indeed stayed for a time. However, the litigant was subsequently able to raise the money and the proceedings were resumed.

References and Further Reading

1. Wilkinson Michael, Booth Christine, Cheung Eric. *The Student Guide to Civil Procedure in Hong Kong*, 2nd edn. LexisNexis 2005; Chapter 20, pp 812-854.

VI

The Medical Council

81

The Medical Council or the court?

We read or hear about Medical Council judgments every now and then and we also hear about court decisions. Which cases are which? How is it determined which case belongs to which body?

This requires an explanation of the role of the Medical Council.

The Hong Kong Medical Council is established under the Medical Registration Ordinance, Chapter 161 of the Laws of Hong Kong. The Council's functions cover the **registration** of medical practitioners, the conduct of the **Licensing** Examination and the maintenance of **ethics**, professional **standards** and **discipline** in the profession. The latter is detailed in the Code of Professional Conduct maintained and regularly updated by the Council itself.

The Medical Registration Ordinance also confers disciplinary powers to the Council. The two most common disciplinary offences are conviction of an **offence punishable with imprisonment** and **misconduct in a professional respect**. The disciplinary powers include: removal from the Register, indefinitely or for a specified period, immediate or suspended; reprimand; and warning in writing. Thus, the Council sees its overall role as both the maintenance of public confidence in the profession and the upholding of the integrity of the profession.

The Medical Council is thus a statutory entity which exists for the purpose of **self-regulation** of the members of the profession. This is in line with the traditional English approach to the regulation of professional bodies in general because there is a presumption that the members of a profession know best how to handle matters of discipline within itself. In this way the approach could be seen as a respect for the profession in the sense that its members are allowed an opportunity to be judged by its own peers instead of by the 'lay' court.

Apart from the statutorily defined functions of registration, licensing and disciplinary regulation of the profession, any other matters are strictly outside the scope of the Medical Council's **jurisdiction** and will default back to the court system. In fact, any appeal from a decision of the Medical Council is to the Court of Appeal, if leave for such is given.

It should now be evident why negligence claims from patients will not be handled by the Medical Council unless there is an element of disciplinary offence. In any event, the Medical Council has no power to award compensation.

References and Further Reading

1. The website of the Medical Council of Hong Kong at http://www. mchk.org.hk/.
2. The Hong Kong Medical Council Professional Code and Conduct 1994.
3. The Hong Kong Medical Council Code of Professional Conduct 2009.

82

Role of the Medical Council

The Medical Council of Hong Kong is a statutory body under the Medical Registration Ordinance, Chapter 161 of the Laws of Hong Kong, established for the purpose of regulating the professional conduct of registered medical practitioners in Hong Kong. As stated on its web page, it was founded to 'to assure and promote **quality** in the medical profession in order to **protect** patients, foster **ethical conduct**, and develop and maintain high professional **standards**'.

Its functions include:
- Registration of medical practitioners and maintenance of the list of medical practitioners;
- Maintenance of the list of quotable qualifications;
- Licensing matters including the licentiate examination;
- Maintenance of the Code of Professional Conduct; and,
- Conducting disciplinary inquiries and hearings.

Is the Code of Professional Conduct law? The author often hears of comments by colleagues that the Code is not law. True. It is not. However, it is wrong at the same time to regard the Code as not having the **effect of law**. It does. Although the Code is not legislation and has not gone through the legislative process of bill proposal, first, second and third readings, etc, it comprises self-regulatory rules provided by the Council, which has been empowered by the law to discipline the profession. In this way, the Code's effect is actually no different from the law itself when applied to practitioners within its ambit.

The Code does change with time, as does the law. When considered outdated, or where further clarification becomes necessary, the clauses are amended, deleted or new ones added. In January 2009, a new Code of

Professional Conduct was released replacing the previous Professional Code and Conduct of 1994 (revised in November 2000), which, in turn, was preceded by a Warning Notice of 1957. The new Code is an updated version. It is more comprehensive in scope as well as more detailed and specific with respect to some issues. The Code aims at maintaining high professional standards and fostering ethics in practice. The Code is, however, not meant to be exhaustive and it is explicitly mentioned in Part I Section A that interpretation should be in the **purposeful** sense in order to attain the spirit behind the provisions of the Code.

Every medical practitioner is provided with a copy of the Code on first registration and amendments to the Code are disseminated by mail as well as through the Council's newsletters.

In the author's experience, it is surprisingly uncommon for busy doctors to look at and check the Code. However, in view of the regulatory role of the Council and its Code perusal is very much advisable in order to avoid inadvertent infringements.

References and Further Reading

1. Medical Registration Ordinance, Chapter 161 of the Laws of Hong Kong.
2. The website of the Medical Council of Hong Kong at http://www.mchk.org.hk/.
3. The Hong Kong Medical Council Professional Code and Conduct 1994.
4. The Hong Kong Medical Council Code of Professional Conduct 2009.

83

What offences would count?

The natural reaction for a careful medical practitioner would be what offences would the Medical Council look at? Certainly not every little offence matter or we all have to start worrying.

'Conviction of an offence **punishable with imprisonment**' is the criterion under Part II of the 1994 Professional Code and Conduct. In the 2009 Code of Professional Conduct, this is under Section H, 'Criminal Conviction and Disciplinary Proceedings'.

'**Punishable**' implies that an offender is caught by the rule even if he is not actually taken into prison, such as when he is not so sentenced or merely given a suspended sentence, etc. Conviction is the trigger irrespective of actual imprisonment. Convictions both inside and outside the HKSAR are counted. The Council, however, may decide that no inquiry is necessary where the conviction is not considered to affect the doctor's practice as a registered medical practitioner.

Paragraph 29 imposes a **duty to report**. A registered practitioner so convicted thus has a duty to report the conviction to the Medical Council within 28 days of the conviction, failure of which is grounds for disciplinary action. In the event that one is not sure whether an offence is punishable with imprisonment, it is better to report it for the Council to sort it out.

It is also stated that a particularly serious view is taken of offences involving **dishonesty**, **indecent behaviour** or **violence**, Paragraph 27.2.

Section 20A(2) of the Medical Registration Ordinance, Chapter 161 of the Laws of Hong Kong, stipulates the requirement for **evidence of no conviction** in the application of a practising certificate by a registered medical practitioner. This is usually in the form of a declaration.

One interesting question affecting many of us is whether a minor traffic offence, such as speeding or illegal parking, is included? Most doctors drive for the advantage of time and convenience and it is inevitable that sooner or later they will receive tickets or letters of intention to prosecute from the police. Fortunately for us in the profession, the answer is no. This is because a **fixed penalty** under the Fixed Penalty (Criminal Proceedings) Ordinance, Chapter 240, is not considered a conviction.

References and Further Reading

1. Medical Registration Ordinance, Chapter 161 of the Laws of Hong Kong.
2. The website of the Medical Council of Hong Kong at http://www.mchk.org.hk/.
3. The Hong Kong Medical Council Professional Code and Conduct 1994.
4. The Hong Kong Medical Council Code of Professional Conduct 2009.
5. Fixed Penalty (Criminal Proceedings) Ordinance, Chapter 240 of the Laws of Hong Kong.

84

What constitutes 'Professional Misconduct'?

Also referred to as 'misconduct in a professional respect', the term 'professional misconduct' has been defined by the Medical Council of Hong Kong in the 1994 Professional Code and Conduct as:

'If a medical practitioner in the pursuit of his profession has done something which will be reasonably regarded as **disgraceful**, **unethical** or **dishonourable** by his professional colleagues of good repute and competency, then it is open to the Medical Council of Hong Kong, if that be shown, to say that he has been guilty of professional misconduct.'

We are fortunate now to have, since January 2009, the new revised Code of Professional Conduct as that sheds further light on the issue. The new version has this:

'The term "misconduct in a professional respect" is not defined in the Medical Registration Ordinance but has been interpreted by the Court of Appeal as conduct **falling short of the standards expected** among registered medical practitioners. It includes not only conduct involving **dishonesty** or **moral turpitude**, but also any act, whether by commission or omission, which has fallen **below the standards of conduct which is expected** of members of the profession. It also includes any act which is reasonably regarded as disgraceful, dishonourable or unethical by medical practitioners of good repute and competency.'

The Code of Professional Conduct sets out various kinds of professional misconduct which may lead to disciplinary proceedings by the Council. It has to be remembered that that is NOT a complete or exhaustive listing of all the forms of disciplinary misconduct.

The reader is reminded again of the importance of this document and to refer to the Code for its details, which are clearly, precisely and eloquently expressed in simple plain English.

References and Further Reading

1. The Hong Kong Medical Council Professional Code and Conduct 1994.
2. The Hong Kong Medical Council Code of Professional Conduct 2009.

85

Colleagues practicing inappropriately

This is an area of serious conflict and, very often, embarrassment.

The Declaration of Geneva says, '… my colleagues will be my brothers… '. In The International Code of Medical Ethics, we have, 'A physician shall behave towards colleagues as he/she would have them behave towards him/her.'

At the same time, under The International Code of Medical Ethics, a physician shall 'respect the local and national codes of ethics', he shall also 'deal honestly with patients and colleagues, and report to the appropriate authorities those physicians who practice unethically or incompetently or who engage in fraud or deception'. Further, under The Declaration of Geneva, a physician on being admitted to the profession affirms, 'I will maintain by all the means in my power, the honour and the noble traditions of the medical profession… '.

How is it ever justified to report a colleague suspected of malpractice or inappropriate practice? The conclusion is now clear. Although reporting a malpractising colleague is a conduct against your colleague, the duty to uphold the integrity and reputation of the profession prevails.

Having said that, a physician suspecting malpractice and intending to report a colleague must first evaluate how strong the evidence is. Mere speculation without convincing evidence may simply expose oneself to a counterclaim of defamation. It might be necessary to do some research and gathering of facts. Discussion with the committee members of one's professional society may be helpful. Often it is advisable to seek legal advice before action is undertaken.

An analogy here might perhaps better illustrate the point. A friend of 20 years has recently killed an innocent person. Should you report him to the police? Would you rather cherish the friendship just to see him do the same again? Is our responsibility to a friend more important or our duty to society? It is a dilemma but the answer should be simple enough to arrive at.

This is not to create a culture of mutual criticism and condemnation. It is perhaps better to see this as a means of self-regulation of a highly regarded profession and as a mechanism for the maintenance of the trust the public has confided in us. We are the members of an authoritative circle and only very stringent discipline will safeguard the confidence and respect that we enjoy.

References and Further Reading

1. The Hong Kong Medical Council Professional Code and Conduct 1994.
2. The Hong Kong Medical Council Code of Professional Conduct 2009.

__VII__

Death

86

'Do Not Resuscitate'

In 2007, the British Medical Association and the Royal College of Nursing issued a joint set of guidelines on decision-making relating to cardio-pulmonary resuscitation (CPR).

The guidelines emphasise that:

- an informed, non-coerced, advance directive must be respected;
- in the absence of such, the presumption should be in favour of attempting resuscitation;
- views of the relatives of incompetent adults must be taken into account but their role is not to take decisions on behalf of the patient;
- adequate documentation of the decisions must be made including how they were reached;
- non-treatment decisions in the incapacitated should normally be taken by health professionals in concert with people close to the patient; and,
- recourse is to the courts if there is disagreement.

Ultimately, to enable '**dying with dignity**' is an integral part of medical treatment and a basic duty of a responsible clinician.

It is also not to be forgotten that a 'do not resuscitate' form may not be valid when signed without a thorough explanation or if out-dated.

References and Further Reading

1. *Decisions Relating to Cardiopulmonary Resuscitation.* British Medical Association, the Resuscitation Council (UK) and the Royal College of Nursing 2007 available at website: http://www.bma.org.uk/images/DecisionsRelatingResusReport_tcm41-147300.pdf.

87

Substitute decision-making

A person may have preferences as to what he would like to have done to his body by medical practitioners when he is no longer able to indicate those wishes in the **terminal** stages of his illness. A colleague of the author used to stress that he would not want needles and puncture holes in his heart and young energetic doctors fracturing his ribs before he was allowed to die.

Can one ensure his 'will' in such a context?

Two terms are becoming important to the medical practitioner. **Substitute decision-making** refers to decisions as to medical treatment being made on behalf of a patient by someone else, such as a doctor, when the patient is in coma or in a vegetative condition. **Advance directive** is the situation where the patient himself, while competent, gives instructions as to the medical treatment he wishes to receive if he later becomes incompetent to make such a decision.

At the time of writing, the status of development in Hong Kong in this area is only that of a set of proposals in a report published in 2006 by the Hong Kong Law Reform Commission, a body which reviews and advises on the update of the law. The Commission recommended that the Government promote public awareness and understanding of the concepts, and to consider legislation in due course.

The concern to most doctors will obviously be whether the instructions in an advance directive or in substitute decision-making are valid. This will not only be very much dependent on how the law is drafted but also whether the statutory forms and procedural requirements involved are observed and fulfilled.

References and Further Reading

1. Kenyon Mason, Alexander McCall Smith, and Graeme Laurie. *Law and Medical Ethics*, 6th edn. LexisNexis Butterworths 2002; Chapters 16 and 17.

—— 88 ——

Euthanasia

Euthanasia refers to the **premature termination of life** for the purposes of a 'better death'. Up to the present, the law in both the United Kingdom and in Hong Kong does not allow euthanasia. The basis of this of course lies in the fundamental respect for human life and the profession's role to help rather than to destroy.

Euthanasia can be **voluntary** or involuntary. Where a terminally ill patient specifically requests that his life be ended, it is voluntary euthanasia. **Non-voluntary** euthanasia involves the avoidance of undue suffering of someone who can no longer express any views and whose position is therefore ascertained by reference to the family or the medical attendant, usually for non-treatment.

Euthanasia can also be classified as active and passive.

There is no doubt that a positive and **active** act of euthanasia is illegal if done with intention to kill and does, in fact, kill. Motive is irrelevant in the law and if a doctor intends to kill, he is as liable to prosecution as is the layman, irrespective of the fact that he is a genuine 'mercy-killer'. Whether doctors can lawfully 'provide the means of ending life to a patient who will complete the act' is still in doubt. In *Rodriquez v A-G of British Columbia* (1993), a case considered by the Supreme Court of Canada, a patient with motor neurone disease wished to have in place a mechanism to self-termination of her life when she became paralysed. The court decided that State prohibitions that would force a dreadful, painful death on a rational but incapacitated terminally ill person would be an affront to human dignity. Despite this decision, further authorities must be awaited.

Passive euthanasia involves the shortening of life through an omission to act, such as the withholding of life-sustaining treatment in a terminal patient. Selective non-treatment is common.

In this connection, the author agrees with authorities advocating the distinction between withholding and withdrawal of treatments. The former is passive and the latter active. Schools of thought mingling the two inevitably come to the conclusion that they have to dispense with the distinction between active and passive euthanasia as well, because the two become difficult to separate.

English criminal law distinguishes sharply between acts as to whether they are commissions or omissions. An act causing death without lawful excuse and with intent to kill is murder, but an **omission to act** with the same result and intent is not an offence. The latter is subject to the proviso that one is not under a duty to act, and here it means that the omission is covered by good medical practice.

One interesting issue is the **principle of double effect**. This means that an act with a good objective is allowed despite a coincident harmful effect, provided that the good effect outweighs the bad. The seminal case is *R v Adams* (1957). Dr. Adams was alleged to have killed an incurable patient with opiates. He was tried for murder and was acquitted. The court said: 'The doctor is entitled to relieve pain and suffering even if the measures he takes may incidentally shorten life.' This direction was followed in *R v Cox* (1993) and cited with approval by the House of Lords in *Airedale NHS Trust v Bland* (1993): '… a doctor may… [in a] patient who is… dying of cancer, lawfully administer painkilling drugs despite… an incidental effect… to abbreviate the patient's life… '

To summarise, the law clearly prohibits two situations:

- Positive acts with the principal intention of terminating life; and,
- Assisted suicide, as distinct from suicide.

It may be of interest to the reader as well to look into how the Netherlands, where medical euthanasia became lawful in 2000, deals with the issue. The Termination of Life on Request and Assisted Suicide

(Review Procedures) Act, Article 293 amends the Penal Code of the Netherlands to read:

> (2) The offence... shall not be punishable if it has been committed by a physician who has met the requirements of due care [referred to in Article 2 of this law]... who informs the municipal autopsist of this...

Due care is defined as requiring that the request was 'voluntary and well considered' and that the suffering was 'lasting and unbearable'. There must have been no other reasonable solution. An independent physician is also required to see the patient to give a written opinion on compliance with due conditions. Nearly 2 per cent of deaths in the Netherlands results from euthanasia.

References and Further Reading

1. Kenyon Mason, Alexander McCall Smith, and Graeme Laurie. *Law and Medical Ethics*, 6th edn. LexisNexis Butterworths 2002; Chapter 18.
2. *Rodriquez v A-G of British Columbia* (1993) 82BCLR 2d 273.
3. *R v Adams* (1957) Crim LR 365.
4. *R v Cox* (1993) 12 BMLR 38.
5. *Airedale NHS Trust v Bland* (1993) 1 All ER 821.
6. The (Netherlands) Termination of Life on Request and Assisted Suicide (Review Procedures) Act.

89

Quality of death

This is an often confused topic and it is important to a cautious medical practitioner to be quite clear what quality of death is and what euthanasia is.

Euthanasia is medical assistance in the peaceful passing away of a patient in terminal illness where death is inevitable. It may be active, which is illegal in most parts of the world as yet, or, passive, meaning withholding necessary treatment usually in the form of vital support like hydration, nutriment, or ventilatory assistance.

Quality of death is a totally different issue. By this term we mean the maintenance of a reasonable or acceptable or at the very least a more respectable level of quality of life in patients approaching death. Of course it is in comparison to the level of quality of life one would expect were intervention not given. Thus, most medical practitioners are already giving one kind of treatment or another in their attempts to help alleviate the pains of death. We all conventionally call this **palliation**.

Examples of such endeavours abound and it is easy to cite a few. Dysphagia from obstructing tumours could be by-passed with stents or relieved using laser ablation. Pain may be suppressed by the anaesthetist with pain management expertise. Ulcerating and messy wounds on the body could be better handled with excision and flap coverage and specialised nursing care.

Yet, it should never be overlooked that we are at the centre of a team in our medical strategies and we are not the only means of resort. Thus, depressive moods could require the input of a counsellor or a religious representative, in addition to the expertise of a psychiatrist. Expert nursing care can often improve significantly the immediate environment the patient is to be in. Supporting relatives are an immensely important source of relief to the dying. Engagement therapy could be in the form of appropriate exercises or mental occupation.

We should always consider helping our dying patients to suffer as little as possible by providing symptom control, comfort care and emotional support. That is a part of our duties as a medical practitioner.

References and Further Reading

1. Kenyon Mason, Alexander McCall Smith, and Graeme Laurie. *Law and Medical Ethics*, 6th edn. LexisNexis Butterworths 2002; Chapters 16-18.

90

Medical futility

The term medical futility may not be new to the up-to-date reader but it was certainly not a widely discussed topic until a decade or so ago. Obviously there are a lot of controversies about many aspects of the concept and the author is not attempting to resolve them or to take sides in this discussion. One sure observation is that the medical practitioner is no longer to be regarded as an instrument of healing without at the same time exercising judgment. There exists a line beyond which we should acknowledge our limitations and wave the white flag.

Medical futility refers to **medical interventions which are not effective** in achieving medical benefits or meeting the patient's goals. Where a particular intervention known to date to the profession cannot provide a minimum likelihood of benefit, it is not owed to the patient as a matter of moral duty.

It should be clear here that we are not talking about euthanasia under the head of futility. The topic is not concerned with any **external agency of death** but how a patient should be left to die. This latter point, if overlooked, will lead to confusion as to one's understanding and approach.

Very often the issue centres on the **continual administration of supportive care** to the dying, such as artificial ventilation, tube feeding, intravenous support of fluids, cardiac support, etc. The case law in this area is illustrative of the court's approach and has mainly been concerned with the management of the patient in a 'persistent vegetative state' (PVS).

The first important and most famous is *Airedale NHS Trust v Bland* (1993). Bland was crushed by crowds in a football stadium and sustained severe anoxic brain damage. Three years later, he remained in a PVS and the hospital sought a declaration to lawfully discontinue supportive measures. This was granted and the court clarified that treatment was governed by necessity in the patient's best interests. Without hope of recovery, interest in being kept alive and necessity both disappear, and therefore the duty to act was gone. There is thus no crime in omitting to act.

In *Frenchay Healthcare NHS Trust v S* (1994), the gastrostomy tube of a young man who had been in a PVS for two and a half years from drug overdose slipped. Declaration for withholding supportive treatment was again granted and this was upheld on appeal. The test used was again the patient's best interests. The test, that the doctor's decision is to be judged against one which would be taken by a responsible and competent body of relevant professional opinion, is also confirmed to be applicable in deciding whether a decision is in the patient's best interests.

The court in *NHS Trust A v Mrs M, NHS Trust B v Mrs H* (2001) referred to the 'responsible body of medical opinion' approach as the '**good faith' approach**. In this case, the issue was also examined from the perspective of fundamental **human rights** as the trial was heard after the Human Rights Act 1998. It was reconfirmed that the court had to be the final arbiter of best interests for the purpose of Article 2 (right to life) of the Act. Article 3 (prohibition against cruel and inhuman treatment) was not infringed as there is no capacity to experience it. As for Article 8 (respect for private life), the court considered continuation of treatment against the patient's interests instead was a violation.

This topic is for sure evolving and the reader will be participating in and contributing to its development.

References and Further Readings

1. Kenyon Mason, Alexander McCall Smith, and Graeme Laurie. *Law and Medical Ethics*, 6th edn. LexisNexis Butterworths 2002; Chapters 16 and 17.
2. *Airedale NHS Trust v Bland* (1993) 1 All ER 821.

3. *Frenchay Healthcare NHS Trust v S* (1994) 1 WLR 601.
4. *NHS Trust A v Mrs M, NHS Trust B v Mrs H* (2001) 1 All ER 801.
5. The (English) Human Rights Act 1998.
6. *Withholding and Withdrawing Life-prolonging Treatments: Good Practice in Decision-Making* on General Medical Council's website at http://www.gmc-uk.org/guidance/current/library/witholding_lifeprolonging_guidance.asp.

91

Clinical post-mortem or Coroner's Court

Doctors who have been practising for some time will say that post-mortem examination can be in two forms: the clinical post-mortem and the coroner's post-mortem.

This is actually somewhat a misconception of the situation. More accurately speaking, a **post-mortem** is an autopsy requested by the attending doctor of the deceased who wishes to understand more of the death of the latter by further examination of the dead body. A **referral to the coroner**, on the other hand, is a duty imposed by law under the Coroners Ordinance, Chapter 504 of the Laws of Hong Kong.

The indications for a referral to the coroner is listed under '**Reportable Deaths**' as specified in column 2 of Part 2 of Schedule 1 of the Coroners Ordinance. Under section 4(2) of the Ordinance, a person who fails to discharge such a duty commits an offence and is liable on conviction to a fine at level 1 and to imprisonment for 14 days. This latter statutory rule is not widely known to medical practitioners to the author's knowledge and can be a deadly trap to the unwary, because ignorance of the law is never an excuse for an offence. It is hence obvious that one should find out and be familiar with the specific items of Reportable Deaths from the Ordinance.

Whether a referral to the coroner would then end up in a post-mortem depends on the coroner, and it is for the coroner to decide not the referring medical practitioner. Presumably if there is no argument as to the exact cause of death, the coroner may waive an autopsy.

The coroner may also require an **inquest into the death** of the deceased. The purposes of such inquests are limited to the identity of the deceased, the cause of death, the time of death and where the deceased died. No question of civil liability concerns a Coroner's Court, section 44, and such claims are only to be heard through another civil claims proceeding. Where it comes to the coroner's suspicion that in relation to the death of the deceased, a person might have committed a criminal offence such as murder or manslaughter, the coroner will adjourn the proceedings and refer the case to the Secretary for Justice for further action.

The important conclusion is that, if a clinician is simply interested in the medical aspect of the death and wants to have an autopsy, he should speak to the relatives for consent to do so. A referral to the coroner is not to be taken as a way to bypass the refusal of the relatives, nor will it guarantee that an autopsy would be performed.

Before we finish, who can be a coroner? A **coroner** is a qualified barrister or solicitor who has practised for at least 5 years and is appointed by the Chief Executive as such.

References and Further Reading
1.   Coroners Ordinance, Chapter 504 of the Laws of Hong Kong.

VIII

The Profession and Society

92

To whom am I responsible?

Assuming that the reader is a medical practitioner, have you ever thought about this question? Or in the event that the reader is not a medical practitioner, what would you expect in that respect of a doctor?

The author considers that the patient is the centre of a wide scope comprising various **stakeholders** to whom a doctor has a duty of responsibility. In no order of importance, these are:

- The **government** – in terms of the provision of health care services
- The **hospital** – as an employee of that institution
- The **patient** – inherent and central in the doctor-patient relationship
- The **public** – as role models of a healthy lifestyle and education in terms of public health
- Your **teachers** – to honour their dedication in enabling their students to practise medicine to help people
- The medical **students** and junior doctors – in passing on medical knowledge and providing training opportunities
- The **doctor** himself – to be a respectable professional so as to be proud of his efforts
- The **profession** – to uphold the reputation and noble tradition of the profession
- **God** – if a follower of a faith
- **Human kind** – to do good for your fellow man

A doctor may find his role differs compared with that of a colleague, depending on his specialty and his position. Ultimately, the final test is perhaps what you suppose the reasonable **legitimate expectations** of the people in society around you are of your role. If those expectations can be met you are most likely on the right professional track.

References and Further Reading
1. *Duties of a Doctor* under *Good Medical Practice* on the General Medical Council's website at http://www.gmc-uk.org/guidance/good_medical_practice/duties_of_a_doctor.asp.

93

Moral duty versus legal duty

It might easily appear to an ordinary person that what is moral must be legal and vice versa, because they are both inclined towards the good side of things.

In reality, this is not absolutely the case.

It might be interesting to cite the example of a real incident. A man owning a transport business suffered a severe attack of angina and collapsed. He was driven in a truck by his son and business partner to a nearby hospital. They knew how to get to the hospital but because of the size of their vehicle they went to the main entrance rather than straight to the Accident and Emergency Department. The son tried to carry his father into the hospital but could only get him to the side of the road where he started manual cardio-pulmonary resuscitation. Meanwhile, the business partner went to seek help at the hospital's enquiry counter, expecting some kind of action, only to be told that the proper thing to do was to dial the emergency number '999'.

Not unexpectedly, a public scandal followed with the media and the public criticising the hospital and its administration and claiming the response was inappropriate.

Analysing the legal standpoint in what happened, it is clear that no doctor-patient relationship had ever been started. In any event, the man did receive almost immediate professional treatment from a doctor who was passing by and the cause of the man's death was hence not attributable to the hospital's refusal to act. In other words, it is arguable that the hospital did not owe the gentleman a duty of care and the man's death would not have been avoidable even had the hospital taken more positive immediate action. The causation of any damage suffered could therefore not be attributed to the hospital.

Despite being in such a safe **legal position**, there was an important lesson to be learnt by the hospital and its administration. More is always expected morally than legally. The reason for this is simple. If the standard required by the law was too strict, the law could be seen as too harsh. Thus, a person on the street can stand and watch a crime taking place without taking any action to help and yet not commit any offence in the law, because he has no duty to assist in the first place. From the **moral perspective**, however, it is arguable that one should always play one's part, as a responsible citizen, in the attempt to fight crime in an appropriate situation.

The lesson is therefore to distinguish clearly what standard one should be using before action is taken. Failure to do so and **adopting the wrong standard** in a particular scenario can lead to very diverse and unexpected outcomes.

The relationship between moral duty and legal duty was eloquently expressed in a most accurate manner in the case of *R v Instan* (1893), in which Lord Chief Justice Coleridge said, 'It would not be correct to say that every moral obligation involves a legal duty; but every legal duty is founded on a moral obligation.'

References and Further Reading

1.   *R v Instan* (1893) 1 QB at 453.

94

Good practice versus legal requirement

It is increasingly common to come across the term 'good medical practice' these days and guidelines for what constitutes good medical practice are regularly issued by authoritative professional bodies such as the General Medical Council.

It may be useful to be clear in one's mind the purpose for stating what is good medical practice. Good practice is, as its name suggests, what is regarded as good in medical practice. To be 'good' often actually implies a degree of 'better' practice in the presence of alternative ways of doing things.

Many a time good practice incorporates what is legally required. Indeed, good practice often exceeds **legal requirements** and goes further with a view to the better management of patients.

The point is best clarified by an example again. Patients often default appointments for investigations for one reason or another. Let's say it's a colonoscopy examination where a patient is to be admitted as a day case for the procedure. The patient fails to turn up. What are the duties of the hospital in tracing the patient? What would be the hospital's liability for not doing anything to recall the patient? What if the patient turned out to have a colonic cancer and diagnosis and treatment were delayed as a result of the default? The truth of the matter is that the patient has every right not to turn up. He has the full right to go to any other doctor or institution. He has the full right to come back later for an appointment if he chooses to do something else in the meantime which he considers more urgent. Should his default cause his demise, he is to be blamed. Such was the immediate cause of any resulting damage and the caring doctors should be safe from reproach, provided that they have explained, to the patient's understanding, the indications and necessity for the investigation.

On the other hand, had the hospital been diligent enough to trace the patient and to remind him of the appointment and to advise him to return for further work-up that would be considered good medical practice.

To sum up, good medical practice is in a way doing **more than obligatory** in order to provide a better and safer service. It is something in line with our much valued modern culture of quality and exceeding expectations as well as process re-engineering for continuous improvement.

We are certainly prepared as professionals to do our best and to do more than what the law requires. The latter should only prescribe the minimal standard of tolerance below which some form of prohibition and penalty becomes mandatory.

References and Further Reading

1. *Good Medical Practice* on the General Medical Council's website at http://www.gmc-uk.org/guidance/good_medical_practice/index. asp.

95

Accidents on the road

The author can still recall vividly one occasion when he was a medical student attending a forensic medicine lecture. When the lecture was over, the lecturer remained to chat with the class.

The lecturer was telling us students never to stop if driving by a road accident and not to be heroic in going out to help, proclaiming that you are a doctor coming to give assistance. His rationale was that since equipment would be lacking and help nowhere about there would be no guarantee of being able to do an adequate job. One thus exposes oneself unnecessarily to potential litigation by the injured if he later finds out that something which the doctor could have done he had either not done or not done well.

This 'teaching' has since puzzled the author as conflicting with the role of a responsible doctor in society. To say the least, it is a most vivid example of '**defensive medicine**', and of course it is always the safest practice not to practise at all!

The author was and is not in agreement with this doctrine or attitude. Is there a legal duty to help? Strictly speaking the answer is no. This is because the law imposes duties not to cause damage to, but not actively to help, others. However, being a professional medical man, it cannot be denied that there is a **moral as well as an ethical obligation** to assist.

The Hippocratic Oath in its second principle says, 'To practise and prescribe to the best of my ability for the good of my patients, and to try to avoid harming them.' The fifth principle has it, 'To keep the good of the patient as the highest priority.' It is difficult to see how sneaking away from the scene could be compatible with these duties.

Similarly, The Declaration of Geneva reads, 'At the time of being admitted as a member of the medical profession: I solemnly pledge myself to consecrate my life to the service of humanity… I will practise my profession with conscience and dignity… I will maintain by all the means in my power, the honour and the noble traditions of the medical profession… I will maintain the utmost respect for human life… '.

In the 2006 version of Good Medical Practice published by the General Medical Council of the United Kingdom, the list of duties of a doctor starts with '… you must show respect for human life… '

It is also worthwhile to recall that Medical Protection Society membership protects against Good Samaritan acts irrespective of where action is brought.

Having said this, it is also important to remember that a duty of care exists once care is assumed and the doctor-patient relationship starts. The doctor is therefore susceptible to negligence claims. There are presently proposals, notably by the Irish Law Reform Commission, as to a full defence against civil liability for Good Samaritans and **voluntary rescuers**, unless there is gross negligence.

It might be interesting to know why a volunteer rescuer has come to be known as a **Good Samaritan**. The origin of this label is in the New Testament of the Bible, where in the Gospel of St. Luke Jesus used the Parable of the Good Samaritan to illustrate that we should show human kindness and feeling towards our fellow men and neighbours.

'Love your neighbour as yourself… ' A man was going down from Jerusalem to Jericho, when he fell into the hands of robbers. They stripped him of his clothes, beat him and went away, leaving him half dead with no clothes. A priest happened to be going down the same road, and when he saw the man, he passed by on the other side. So too, a Levite, when he came to the place and saw him, he passed by on the other side. But a Samaritan, as he travelled, came where the man was; and when he saw him, he took pity on him. He went to him and bandaged his wounds, pouring on oil and wine. Then he put the man on his own donkey, took him to an inn and took care of him. The next day he took out two silver coins and gave them to the innkeeper. 'Look after him,' he said, 'and when I return, I will reimburse you for any extra expense you may have.' 'Which of these three do you think was a neighbour to the man who fell into the hands of robbers?' The expert in the law replied, 'The one who had mercy on him.' Jesus told him, 'Go and do likewise.' (Luke 10.25-37.)

References and Further Reading

1. The Hippocratic Oath.
2. The Declaration of Geneva.
3. *Good Medical Practice* on the General Medical Council's website at http://www.gmc-uk.org/guidance/good_medical_practice/index.asp.
4. The Bible: the Gospel according to St. Luke 10.25-37.

——— 96 ———

Tied hand and foot

With so many rules and regulations, items of codes of practice, guidelines, standing orders, good practice, ethics and the law, are we bound hand and foot?

Why should we, as professional people, submit to all these restrictions and strictures?

Is there any infringement on the grounds of our inalienable fundamental human rights?

Is the autonomy of the profession being trampled upon?

Are there justifications for these interventionist sanctions?

The answer is to be found in the well-known 'excuse', the '**public interest**', i.e. that the need is there all because the interests of the public require it.

Why? The medical profession is conferred from ancient times a very high prestige, given superior authority and endowed with practically unsurpassed **autonomy**. No wonder there have to be sufficient checks and balance mechanisms in place. Liberty is thus to be allowed only with the appropriate safeguards. Moreover, the profession is possessed of the power to handle matters directly related to human life. A little more control is, from this perspective, justifiable and with very good cause.

The situation is thus analogous to the concept propounded by '**social contract**' theorists. Protection is provided in return for suitable controls. We enjoy a high degree of independence and so we should be subject to a corresponding degree of discipline.

97

Managed care

Managed care refers to health care delivery systems that contractually link employers and patients with medical services provider organisations. They often strive to achieve cost-containment through education and prevention and control measures geared at the primary care level. The managed care system has become more important as a model of health care delivery as a result of escalating medical costs over the past few decades.

Because medical treatments are sanctioned, and incentives or penalties are employed by health plan managers to influence medical services utilisation, a potential conflict exists in relation to the duty of care of providers towards patients and their obligations to the health management organisations (HMOs).

For example, there have been reported tactics which were arguably against the doctors' ethical duty in attempts towards cost-containment by some organisations:

- Encouraging forced 'drive-through' (one-day stay) hospital procedures such as deliveries and mastectomies;
- Giving doctors economic incentives for denial of care;
- Imposing 'gag' orders in the provision of some treatment options;
- Enforcing the use of unnecessary investigations for financial gain; and,
- Allowing administrative decisions to influence or override medical decisions.

The point to note from the medical practitioners' perspective is their independence as clinicians. Clinical autonomy must never be compromised for considerations of fiscal policies or profit making for the organisation. The patient and his interests should always be the first and only consideration in medical decision making. Quality care is always from the customer's point of view not that of the organisation. The professional duty of care is towards the patient no matter what is written in the contract of employment.

Recent studies have confirmed the view that HMOs are assuming an important position in the provision of primary health care in Hong Kong. Similarly, various associations and bodies, and not the least the medical profession itself, are calling for amendment of existing legislation to bring the regulation of HMOs under the jurisdiction of the Medical Council.

The medical profession must monitor closely the rapid changes in this development. In the event, should the Government establish a commission to overlook the situation, doctors must secure a strong representation on it to ensure our professional autonomy so that a high standard of care can be maintained for patients.

References and Further Reading

1. The Hippocratic Oath.
2. The Declaration of Geneva.
3. Wong CY. *Who manages managed care?* Singapore Medical Association News 2008; 40: 5-7.
4. Law CL. *Managed Care and HMO – the Basics.* Hong Kong Academy of Medicine website at http://www.hkam.org.hk/temp/hmo.html.
5. Yuen P. *An Analysis of the Managed Care Market in Hong Kong.* Public Policy Research Institute, the Hong Kong Polytechnic University 2007 available at: http://www.bauhinia.org/publications/BFRC-MCO-Report.pdf.

98

General approach in decision-making in ethical issues

When it comes to difficult situations when a medical practitioner is faced with issues of ethical concern, it often puzzles even the somewhat experienced as to what the most appropriate course of action should be.

What follows is the general outline of an approach which may be worth adopting.

- Further patient **counselling** – Talk repeatedly, taking time, employing different members of the medical team, perhaps with the more experienced ones, to seek consensus, if the patient is mentally competent. Help the patient to balance the risks and the benefits in his circumstances to make the most appropriate decision in his interests. It should, however, be remembered that the opinion of a patient with a clear and competent mind prevails over that of the family members. Also, with a patient who is incapable of making decisions, such as with the mentally disabled, the medical team can go ahead with their decision against opposing opinion of the family members if that is certainly in the interests of the patient.

- Recruitment of views of **family** members – Let the family members join hands with the medical team and make sure they understand the views and rationale of the medical decision. Most family members are supportive and this source of support often works well.

- **Independent medical opinion** – When it is a matter of a difficult medical decision in a borderline situation, it may well be wise to gather independent expert opinion from colleagues. Consultations on such a basis need not mean giving away one's patient, unless that is the intention and the party consulted agrees. Another alternative in this situation is to present the case in academic meetings for an open discussion to collect views.

- **Good medical practice** – Various official bodies such as the British Medical Association and the Medical Protection Society publish guidelines on various sensitive topics and these are precious sources of reference to resort to for guidance.
- **Guidelines** in force – Circulars and guidelines may have been issued by the hospital administration on particular areas of practice.
- **Professional Code** and Conduct – The Medical Council of Hong Kong publishes a Professional Code and Conduct. Also, there are interval amendments, guidelines, advice and reminders, and all are available on the website of the Council. These provide a very detailed list of regulations and principles to follow, which are additionally binding on all registered practitioners.
- Hospital **Ethics Committee** – All modern hospitals these days have an ethics committee which could be resorted to for a possible solution to difficult dilemmas.
- Seeking **legal opinion** – Usually this would occur only after exhausting local advice in the immediate hospital setting. Legal advice may include that provided by the indemnity societies, the hospital's legal department, or one's own private lawyer.
- Seeking the **court's declaration** – In areas of major decision, such as the withdrawal of life-sustaining treatment, it may be necessary to seek the court's view for a declaration before further action is taken.

99

Professionalism

This is another true story.

A lady in her 40s came into the out-patient clinic of a public hospital for a follow-up after having had cosmetic laser treatment on her face for syringoma a year before. The latter is a skin condition affecting the eyelids where subtle nodular lesions appear as a result of sweat duct swelling. It is very common in middle-aged ladies.

Without wasting a second, she came straight to the point, 'Doctor, it didn't work at all.'

The doctor, a consultant who was experienced in cosmetic laser treatment but a newcomer to the hospital, looked at the patient and asked gently if she was a nurse. To his disconcertment, the patient replied angrily, 'How's that relevant?' The lady's medical record had three large clear capital letters right at the top of the first page: 'VIP'. They had been hand-written by the previous medical officer who had since left to set up his own practice.

The doctor then proceeded to politely explain, 'If you were a nurse, it would be easier to explain, nothing more.' He continued, 'Your condition is not curable by laser as it will recur within a few months... If we try hard to burn your skin all the way down to the deep dermis to which these lesions extend, scarring could be the result.' The doctor then advised that the condition was benign and, as laser treatment was entirely for short-term cosmesis, no more should be done unless the patient could accept that recurrence was not unexpected.

The patient then queried why if the first doctor regarded it a useful treatment there should be any reason for a different opinion. She refused the explanation of the doctor and demanded another session of laser!

The doctor then patiently explained that it would be wrong for him to subject her to a treatment which he considered unable to meet her request. In a very rude tone, the patient immediately retorted, 'I don't see how you are able to overrule the opinion of another doctor. I think my Dr. X is more experienced than you!' She continued, 'I've been waiting hours for this consultation and I demand laser treatment!'

The poor new consultant, knowing he had to behave professionally, continued to suppress his natural reactions and said, 'You see, present day laser technology can at most produce a temporary improvement in your case. If we press hard, the risk of scarring will become serious. The point is not how long you've been waiting but whether the treatment can produce the permanent result you want. A responsible doctor should not carelessly agree to something demanded without a basis just to please a patient. We are not refusing to take care of you. Let me make this suggestion: we'll be pleased to see you again in 2 years and if by then there is a breakthrough in technology, and it is available here, I'll offer it to you.'

The patient immediately countered, 'What if you say the same in 2 years' time? You are just trying to brush me off. I wish to file a complaint! Give me the patient relations office (PRO) number.'

The doctor quietly entered his notes into the computer, taking the opportunity meanwhile to think how to further handle this difficult patient.

After some few minutes of silence, the doctor said, still maintaining a calm tone despite his disappointment and frustration, 'Let me explain again to you. It is my sincerest and honest opinion that present day laser treatment won't be able to meet your expectations. We are very pleased to keep your case open if you are keen to continue to have advice here. We can see you in 2 years' time; technological advances won't come that soon and we don't want you to be coming for nothing.'

'If I do not have a treatment session, I will complain.'

The doctor then picked up the phone and dialled the PRO number. He requested the presence of a relations officer to help resolve the situation. An officer agreed to come.

The patient immediately got up from her chair, 'I'm busy; I can't wait. Now give me the follow-up appointment and the PRO number and I'll make the complaint when I have time.' Snatching the appointment slip rudely from the attending nurse's hands, she turned and disappeared swiftly through the door.

How did the doctor think?

Any person on the street who paid a mere 60 dollars was entitled to come into a public hospital demanding a cosmetic procedure, and if unsuccessful, to rudely and with discourtesy insult the doctor, and then threaten to complain with the intention of maliciously blemishing the doctor's personal file in a manner that was tantamount to blackmail, and then to proceed to leave with a look of victory on her face. What had she to loose? Should that be allowed?

The patient in this case had come to the clinic in the first instance by private lobbying, the knowing someone type of approach, and was actually taking unfair advantage of the position, jumping the queue and enjoying services not really helpful but which she wanted. Do we want this kind of corruptive behaviour in our society?

The complaints system had been abused. Was it there to provide remedies for grievances or primarily to soothe the demands of patients for the sake of the hospital's public relations and image? Who cared how the staff being complained about felt? Indeed, the requisition for an explanation after a complaint often represented a further insult to one's authority and dignity because of having to defend oneself or be presumed guilty without ever any open hearing or cross-examination. Is there no room for natural justice in this setting?

In the situation you think that you must be defective in your people-handling skills. Nobody is interested in your explanation. Would the sensible option next time be to give in?

Upset, depressed, with an inward directed anger, full of regret at not being able to handle things better, having no clear notion of what to do next time the thing same happened, with energy levels suddenly reduced to a minimum, and with colleagues looking at you apparently sympathetically but actually thinking now it's your turn, let us ask ourselves what we're there for.

We are there because we are medical professionals.

We don't resent having to remain calm and polite in the face of ruthless behaviour.

We don't lose our temper or control even when criticised, insulted, or defamed.

We are not lost when others are too mean to pay us our deserved respect.

Why?

Because professional ethics demand it of us.

Doctor, you have been **behaving professionally** and you should be proud of doing so!

100

A health service ombudsman?

In the Legislative Council meeting on 14 January 2009, a 'motion not intended to have legislative effect' was passed concerning the medical and health care profession. The title of the motion was 'Establishing an independent statutory office of the Health Service Ombudsman'.

First of all, what is a '**motion not intended to have legislative effect**'? The Legislative Council Rules of Procedure have the following:

'Through debating motions which are not intended to have legislative effect, Members express their views on issues of public concern or call on the Government to take certain actions. Members may also move motions for the adjournment of the Council for the purpose of discussing a specific issue of urgent public importance (Rule 16(2)) and raising any issue concerning public interest (Rule 16(4)).'

Second, what is an '**ombudsman**'?

The word 'ombudsman' is Swedish meaning representative of the people. The idea of having an ombudsman is to provide an alternative channel of redress in addition to the existing ones such as the courts and tribunals and the Legislative Council going through the relevant Members of the Council. Ombudsmen exist in many countries and are usually specifically responsible for maladministration in the various sectors of the public service.

In the United Kingdom, the office of the Parliamentary Commissioner for Administration undertakes the role of the Health Services Commissioner. Maladministration is the key issue looked at and has been taken as 'bias, neglect, inattention, delay, incompetence, ineptitude, perversity, turpitude, arbitrariness and so on', as it was described by Mr. Richard Crossman, the Minister who originally introduced the legislation. The jurisdiction of the United Kingdom Commissioner for Health Services is under two headings: matters relating to an alleged failure to provide a service that is meant to be provided, and any other action taken by or on behalf of the Health Authority.

On the positive side, the concept provides a blessing to the public as it offers a new **channel for the redress of grievances** from maladministration, which is cheap, accessible and independent. That is potentially a very strong and effective force for the evolution of a transparent and fair health care system.

A significant development in the United Kingdom has been the removal of the statutory **exclusion of clinical judgments** from the scope of the health service ombudsman's investigations in 1996. The implications are vast and there have been oppositions from within the medical profession and the insurance industry for obvious reasons.

Whether the introduction of a health service ombudsman in Hong Kong is necessary at all is thus an issue. Predictably there would be an anticipated potential rise in litigations and the possible encouragement of a 'give-it-a-try' behaviour on the part of **unmeritorious claimants**. The traditional doctor-patient relationship might potentially be at stake and **defensive medicine** could also be an unhealthy side effect from such a move.

We definitely need further deliberation and discussion before we can come to any conclusion at this moment.

References and Further Readings

1.   Hilaire Barnett. *Constitutional and Administrative Law*, 6th edn. Routledge-Cavendish 2006; Chapter 28, pp 797-816.
2.   Council meetings of the Hong Kong Legislative Council at http://www.legco.gov.hk/english/index.htm.

Afterword

An approach to problem solving

There are many good ways of solving problems. Different methods have been proposed by various authorities and the reader may well have developed his own or adapted one for himself.

The following is a suggested way of problem solving which the author learnt during his law studies. It is in wide use in the legal field and one which is highly recommended by many law teachers.

The usual scenario facing one who is to solve a problem is a bunch of facts. The first step is therefore to **list out the facts**. This is usually simple and straightforward.

The second step is to **identify the issues**. This is often the most difficult step because it is easy to pick the wrong issue, miss an important issue or fail to fully realise the significance of an issue. By identifying issues we mean to write out in a simple sentence what the material points are which require our further analysis. There may be more than one issue or even a list of issues.

Next, some of the facts listed earlier will be relevant to the issue under consideration and some irrelevant. Some important facts which are needed may be missing. The next step will involve **grouping the facts** under the various identified issues, together with any facts still to be obtained.

Analysis can now begin, taking the available and relevant facts into consideration. Unavailable facts may be sought and clarified and then incorporated into the analysis, or, assumptions may be made and the analysis **sub-categorised** under each area of possibilities and conclusions derived accordingly. What is particularly helpful at this stage in analysis is what is usually referred to as '**authority**'. That is taken to mean established rules, well-known phenomena and the expectations of a reasonable person, scientific data, published literature, expert opinion, etc. By citing authorities, a **reasoned opinion** is formed.

By now, the analysis will have led to a number of conclusions and taken into account the assumptions of unknown variables. The last step is therefore to determine the most likely case outcome or conclusion, using common sense and likelihood.

A similar approach can be deployed to formulate a persuasive opinion or speech.

An example is helpful here. A laptop belonging to a very senior doctor was found missing from his office on the doctor's floor. The doctor recalled last seeing it on his desk. Nothing similar had occurred on the floor before. On the day of the loss, a number of overseas scholars who had been visiting the unit on attachment left to return to their home countries. The issue here was obviously how it was possible for the thief to have obtained access to the room. However, this was not identified as the issue. No logical reasoning was employed; instead a haphazard rule was suddenly implemented ordering that one of the two access doors to the floor was to be permanently locked to reduce the number of exits for potential thieves!

The result was predictable. The decision had not been based on any logic and it made sense to no one. No one was convinced of its merit and thus no one followed the rule. The better answer was of course for this doctor to have locked his room, which he never did! This unsatisfactory state of affairs was the direct result of a failure to identify the relevant issue.

Glossary

Accomplice (從犯) A person who participates in a crime though not actually committing the crime hands-on.

Admission (of evidence) (證據之接納) Acceptance of a piece of evidence into consideration in a trial deliberation.

Admission (of guilt) (承認有罪) A confession self-incriminating oneself to guilt.

Advance directive (預先指示) Instructions made by an individual in advance for the decisions to be taken in the event of his being unable to make them in the terminal stages of a disease.

Adversarial process (對抗程序) The confrontational encounter between the opposing parties in a trial.

Agent (代理人) The party acting for the principal upon lawful authority from the latter.

Battery (毆打) Physical contact with another person without the latter's approval.

Bona fide (真誠地) In good faith.

Burden of proof (舉證責任) The onus of having to prove guilt in the other party.

But for (若非因) If it were not for.

Canvassing (遊說勸誘) Getting in touch with potential clients to influence them to create business.

Causation (因果關係) A cause which the law regards as valid and material.

Chain of causation (連串的因果關係) The sequence of causes resulting in a particular damage.

Chaperone (伴隨人) A person accompanying medical examinations to act as a witness of the encounter.

Common law (普通法) The law as enunciated by judicial precedents.

Compensation (賠償) Damages awarded for wrong suffered.

Concession (特許) To let go or compromise.

Confidentiality (保密) Keeping information from being released without approval.

Conflict of interests (利益衝突) The self-interest of a party conflicting with his work or the interests of his clients, or the conflict between the interests of different clients under him.

Consent (同意) Approval after deliberation.

Constitution (憲法) The written document of a state which records the basis and principles of its governance, the duties and powers of the government, and the rights of its people.

Contemporaneous evidence (即時紀錄之證據) Evidence recorded at the material time of occurrence of a said event.

Contempt of court (藐視法庭) Disrespect for the court or its orders.

Contract (合約) An agreement between two parties enforceable in law.

Contributory negligence (共同疏忽) Negligence caused by more than one party with pro rata apportionment of damages.

Coroner's inquest (死因裁判官進行的死因研訊) An inquiry held by the coroner about the deceased.

Counterclaim (反申索) Claim made by the defendant in a civil proceeding on the plaintiff.

Covert surveillance (隱蔽性監察) Monitoring of one's activities in a surreptitious manner.

Criminal negligence (刑事疏忽) Negligence to a criminal degree. Same as gross negligence.

Cross-examination (盤問) Examination by the opposing party of one's own witnesses.

Data subject (資料當事人) The individual whose information is collected.

Data user (資料使用者) The party collecting and using the collected information.

Defame/defamation (誹謗) Publication of a statement which lowers the estimation of another or makes others avoid that person.

Direct discrimination (直接歧視) Treating someone unequally on the basis of some criteria.

Duress (威迫) Force of threat or injury.

Duty of care (謹慎責任) An obligation imposed upon a party to exercise a reasonable standard of care.

Equity (衡平法) A body of principles apart from the common law which aims at remedying unconscionability in certain legal contexts.

Euthanasia (安樂死) Termination of life to achieve a better ending.

Examination-in-chief (訊問) The examination of one's own witness(es).

Expert witness (專家證人) A witness with special knowledge assisting the court in resolving matters required in its deliberation to determine a case.

False imprisonment (非法禁錮) Physical territorial restraint without lawful authority or consent.

Fiduciary relationship (受信關係) A relationship where one places complete confidence and trust in another in regard to a particular transaction or business, e.g. due to the latter's superior knowledge.

Fraudulent registration (藉欺詐而註冊) Obtaining registration status by dishonest means.

Gillick-competent (Gillick資格) A minor who is mentally capable of dealing with his or her own affairs in a mature manner.

Gross negligence (嚴重疏忽) Negligence to a criminal degree.

Harassment (騷擾作為) Offensive behaviour disturbing or upsetting another.

Hearsay (傳聞) Evidence that was not actually witnessed but learnt through another party.

Impecunious/Impecuniosity (無錢) Lacking money.

Indecent assault (猥褻侵犯) Sexual advance short of rape.

Indirect discrimination (間接歧視) The consequence of a policy which applies equally to all but with an effect to favour some sub-groups, e.g. due to difficulties of others to meet the criteria.

Infant (未成年人) A minor in law; under 18 years in Hong Kong.

Interlocutory applications (中期申請) Interim proceedings in preparation to the main trial.

Joint and several (共同及各別) Full liability belongs to all concerned responsible parties and the claimant can pursue all or any particular of those parties for the full compensation.

Jointly (liable) (共同有責) All the responsible parties being liable for the full damages.

Jurisdiction (司法管轄權) Authority conferred on a legal body to adjudicate and enforce judgments.

Lacuna in the law (法律漏洞) A gap in existing law with certain issues still unaddressed.

Legal privilege (法律特權) Privilege of the lay client for confidentiality of information released to his lawyer during the course of seeking legal advice, or, communicated to third parties for the dominant purpose of preparing for a litigation.

Legislature (立法機構) The law-making body in a society.

Liability (法律責任) Legal responsibility.

Limitation (in time) (時效期限) The restriction in time before which legal action could be initiated.

Limited registration (有限度註冊) Registration status for overseas doctors meeting the necessary requirements to cater for their employment, e.g. in universities.

Malicious falsehood (惡意虛假) Dishonestly making a false statement to cause harm.

Medical futility (無效的醫療) The argument that where available treatment or intervention cannot help, futile care should be withheld.

Medical negligence (醫療疏忽) Breach of an accepted standard of care to patients by medical personnel.

Minor/minority (未成年人) A person under the age of 18 in law (for Hong Kong).

Necessity (必要) A defence in law for a wrongful or unlawful act committed in order to avoid a greater harm.

Negligence (疏忽) Breach of a reasonable and accepted standard of care.

Negligence claim (疏忽申索) A claim for compensation for damage resulting from a breach of an accepted standard of care to patients by medical personnel.

Neighbour principle (鄰居原則) The fundamental tort principle that one must take reasonable care in one's acts not to cause foreseeable harm to others likely to be affected.

Non est factum (這不是我所簽署的) This is not what I meant to declare.

Nuisance (滋擾) Unreasonable interference with another's use of land or an act which causes offence, annoyance, inconvenience or injury to the public.

Ombudsman (申訴專員) An intermediate person appointed by an organisation or the government to receive complaints and to seek remedies through recommendations for changes.

Ordinance (條例) Statutory law made by a colony.

Pervasive surveillance (普及監視) Monitoring of someone's activities in an extensive manner.

Precedents (先例) Legal principles laid down in past judgments.

Presumption of innocence (無罪推定原則) A person remains innocent until proven guilty.

Principal (主事人) The party conferring authority for an agent to act in a civil case or the primary actor in a criminal case.

Privacy (私隱) Right to keep information about oneself out of the public domain.

Procure (促致) To obtain or bring about.

Professional incest (專業中的亂倫) Having sex with the client within the context of a professional relationship.

Publication (發布) To make something public. Sometimes, letting even one other third person know is sufficient.

Retainer (聘用) The agreement to keep the service of another.

Right to silence (緘默權) The right of an accused to refuse to answer in police interrogations or at a trial.

Sanctioned offers and payments (附帶條款和解提議和付款) A new introduction with the recent civil justice reform in Hong Kong. A defendant may make a 'sanctioned payment' into court in respect of monetary claims or a 'sanctioned offer' in non-monetary claims. A plaintiff may make a 'sanctioned offer' in respect of both kinds of claim. These are attempts to encourage earlier resolution. Failure to accept a sanctioned offer or payment may result in a party being ordered to pay the other party's costs on an indemnity basis with additional interest at an enhanced rate.

Security for costs (訟費保證金) An order for deposition of possible costs in advance in the event of an unsuccessful litigation for a litigant who may be impecunious and from a foreign country.

Severally (liable) (各別法律責任) Each responsible party being liable for the full damages.

Sexual harassment (性騷擾) Offensive behaviour of a sexual nature disturbing or upsetting another.

Solicitation (of business) (生意游説) Loitering and encouraging actions to create business.

Specific discovery (特定透露) An interlocutory procedure to seek disclosure of information held by the opposite party.

Standard of proof (舉證準則) The degree of proof required.

Submission (屈從) Forced into agreeing under threat.

Substitute decision making (替代人作決定) Decision as to medical treatment to be made by another for someone not in a capacity to do so.

Summons (傳訊) Order from the court calling for attendance.

Taxation (of costs) (訟費評定) Estimation of costs by the court.

Tort (侵權行為) A wrong to another's right.

Trespass (to land) (侵入) Intrusion into another's territory without permission.

Ulterior (motive) (別有的動機) For a hidden and unrelated purpose.

Undue influence (不當影響) One party taking advantage of the other as a result of certain relationships or inequality in power, knowledge or status.

Unethical (不道德) Not according to accepted ethics.

Unmeritorious (litigant) (並無成功機會的申索人) Person pursuing legal action without good grounds or convincing evidence.

Vexatious (無理纏擾) Unmeritorious unwarranted litigations more for causing trouble and to threaten.

Vicarious liability (轉承責任) Liability of the employer resulting from that incurred by the employee(s) in the course of their employment.

Without prejudice (無損權利) Information released, in the process of negotiations in a genuine attempt to settle a dispute, for which exclusion can be claimed from the court in subsequent proceedings.

Witness of fact (事實證人) A witness summoned to court to give factual evidence.

List of Reference Materials

1. *A Guide for Doctors on Handling the Media*. Medical Protection Society 2008.
2. *Acting as an Expert Witness* 2008. General Medical Council at GMC website under the List of Ethical Guidance at: http://www. gmc-uk.org/guidance/ethical_guidance/expert_witness_guidance. asp.
3. Albert Chen. *Legal System of the People's Republic of China*. 3rd edition. LexisNexis Butterworths 2004.
4. Alliance for Human Research Protection website at: http://www. ahrp.org/cms/content/view/29/29/.
5. Ambady N, LaPlante D et al. *Surgeon's Tone of Voice: A Clue to Malpractice History*. Surgery 2002; 132(1): 5-9.
6. Birds John, Hird Norma. *Bird's Modern Insurance Law*, 6th edn. Sweet & Maxwell 2004; Chapter 7 Warranties and Conditions, pp 142-166.
7. Bokhary (editor). *Archbold Criminal Law Pleading, Evidence & Practice 2009*. Sweet & Maxwell; Chapter 6 Costs and legal aid in criminal proceedings.
8. *Britain's Legal Systems*. Aspects of Britain series. HMSO 1996.
9. Catherine Elliott, Frances Quinn. *Contract Law*, 3rd edn. Longman 2001; pp 181-184.
10. *Civil Liability for Invasion of Privacy*. The Law Reform Commission of Hong Kong 2004.
11. *Code of Guidance on Expert Evidence: A Guide for Experts and those Instructing Them for the Purpose of Court Proceedings*. Clinical Risk 2002; 8: 60-66.

12. Code of Professional Conduct of the Medical Council of Hong Kong.

13. *Confidentiality FAQs*. General Medical Council 2004 at GMC website under the List of Ethical Guidance at http://www.gmc-uk. org/guidance/current/library/confidentiality_faq.asp.

14. *Confidentiality: Protecting and Providing Information*. General Medical Council 2004 at GMC website under the List of Ethical Guidance at http://www.gmc-uk.org/guidance/ethical_guidance/index.asp.

15. *Consent to Medical and Dental Treatment*. Guardianship Board of Hong Kong 2005.

16. *Consent: Patients and Doctors Making Decisions Together*. General Medical Council 2008 at website under the List of Ethical Guidance at: http://www.gmc-uk.org/guidance/ethical_guidance/consent_guidance/index.asp.

17. Council of Science Editors website at: http://www.council scienceeditors.org/.

18. Council meetings of the Hong Kong Legislative Council at: http://www.legco.gov.hk/english/index.htm.

19. *Decisions Relating to Cardiopulmonary Resuscitation*. British Medical Association, the Resuscitation Council (UK) and the Royal College of Nursing 2007 available at website: http://www.bma.org.uk/images/DecisionsRelatingResusReport_tcm41-147300.pdf.

20. Diana Kloss. *The Duty of Care: Medical Negligence*. British Medical Journal 1984; 289: 66-68.

21. *Disclosures to Protect the Patient or Others*. General Medical Council (2004), para 27.

22. *Duties of a Doctor* under *Good Medical Practice* on the General Medical Council's website at: http://www.gmc-uk.org/guidance/good_medical_practice/duties_of_a_doctor.asp.

23. Elliott C, Quinn Q. *Contract Law*, 3rd edn. Longman 2001; pp 199-201.

24. *Ethical Guidelines in Telemedicine.* Executive Board of the Finnish Medical Association 1997.

25. *Expert Witness Guidance.* British Medical Association 2006 at: www.bma.org.uk/ap.nsf/Content/Expertwitness.

26. *Good Medical Practice* on the General Medical Council's website at: http://www.gmc-uk.org/guidance/good_medical_practice/index.asp.

27. *Guide to Doctors/Dentists: Consent to Medical and Dental Treatment of Mentally Incapacitated Person in the Context of Part IVB & Part IVC, Mental Health Ordinance (Cap. 136).* Guardianship Board of Hong Kong 2006.

28. *Guide to Good Nursing Practice: Physical Restraint.* Nursing Council of Hong Kong 2008, available at website: http://www.nchk.org.hk/practice/physical_restraint_e.pdf.

29. Hilaire Barnett. *Constitutional and Administrative Law*, 6th edn. Routledge-Cavendish 2006; Chapter 28, pp 797-816.

30. Hobma S, Ram P et al. *Effective Improvement of Doctor-Patient Communication: A Randomized Controlled Trial.* Br J Gen Pract 2006; 56(529): 580-587.

31. Hodgin Ray. *Insurance Law: Text and Materials*, 2nd edn. Routledge-Cavendish 2002; Chapter 1 General introduction, pp 26-27; Chapter 8 Claims, p 580.

32. Patrick Chan (editor-in-chief). *Hong Kong Civil Procedure* (The White Book) 2009 Volume 1. Order 62 Costs Second Schedule 62/App/52-62/App/55. Sweet & Maxwell.

33. *Integrity in Practice: A Practical Guide for Medical Practitioners on Corruption Prevention.* ICAC and HKMA.

34. International Committee of Medical Journal Editors website at: http://www.icmje.org/.

35. Kellogg TE. *A Flawed Effort? Legislating on Surveillance in Hong Kong.* Hong Kong Journal: the Quarterly Online Journal about Issues relating to Hong Kong and China 1/2007 available at: www.hkjournal.org/archive/2007_summer/kellogg.htm.

36. Kirsten Miller. *How Safe are Expert Witnesses?* Casebook. Medical Protection Society 2005; 13(2): 25-26.

37. Kirsten Miller. *On Experts and Immunity*. Casebook. Medical Protection Society 2008; 16(3): 7.

38. Law CL. *Managed Care and HMO – the Basics.* Hong Kong Academy of Medicine website at: http://www.hkam.org.hk/temp/ hmo.html.

39. Kenyon Mason, Alexander McCall Smith, and Graeme Laurie. *Law and Medical Ethics*, 6th edn. LexisNexis Butterworths 2002; Chapter 10, pp 309-363.

40. Mauet Thomas, McCrimmon Les. *Fundamentals of Trial Techniques*. Law Book Co of Australasia 2000.

41. McKendrick E. *Contract Law*, 4th edn. Palgrave Law Masters 2000; Chapters 1-6.

42. Medical Council of Hong Kong inquiry judgment MC 2929/4/E and MC 1/2929/4/E, 2009 available on the web at: http://www. mchk.org.hk/docs/STW_20090501.pdf.

43. *Model Guidelines for the Appropriate Use of the Internet in Medical Practice*. Federation of State Medical Boards of the United States, Inc. 2002.

44. *0-18 Years: Guidance for all Doctors* (*2007*) General Medical Council at: http://www.gmc-uk.org/guidance/ethical_guidance/ children_guidance/index.asp.

45. Padfield N. *Criminal Law*, 2nd edn. Butterworths Core Text Series 2000; Chapter 5, pp 101-102.

46. Paul Davies. *Gower and Davies' Principles of Modern Company Law*, 7th edn. Sweet & Maxwell 2003; pp 381-396, 421-424.

47. Paul Nisselle. *Medico-legal Risk Management*. Surgical News of the Royal Australasian College of Surgeons 2009; 10(6): 41.

48. *Privacy: The Regulation of Covert Surveillance.* The Law Reform Commission of Hong Kong 2006.

49. *Professional Boundaries: A Nurse's Guide to the Importance of Appropriate Professional Boundaries.* National Council of the

State Boards of Nursing, USA 2007 available on the web at: https://www.ncsbn.org/Professional_Boundaries_2007_Web.pdf.

50. *Research: The Role and Responsibilities of Doctors.* General Medical Council 2002 at GMC website under the List of Ethical Guidance at: http://www.gmc-uk.org/guidance/current/library/research.asp.

51. Richard Edwards, Nigel Stockwell. *Trusts and Equity*, 5th edn. Longman 2002; pp 248-251.

52. Robert Milstein. Chapter 5: *Duty of Care, Standard of Care and Standards* in *Report on Telemedicine: An International Comparative Analysis of Policy, Regulatory and Medico-legal Obstacles and Solutions.* Department of Human Services (State of Victoria) 1999.

53. Sandy Anthony, Sara Williams. *Drawing the line.* Medical Protection Society 2008; 16(2): 8-10.

54. Sara Williams. *Tangled Web.* Casebook (Asia). Medical Protection Society 2009; 17(2): 8-11.

55. Smith John. *Smith & Hogan Criminal Law*, 9th edn. Butterworths 1999; Chapter 16, pp 536-540.

56. Suresh Nair. *Medical Negligence: Duty of Care.* Singapore Medical Association News 2001; 33(7): 4-5.

57. Taylor Stephen, Emir Astra. *Employment Law.* Oxford 2006; Chapter 9, pp 177-191.

58. Telemedicine Standards and Guidelines. American Telemedicine Association at: http://www.americantelemed.org.

59. The Hong Kong Medical Council Code of Professional Conduct 2009.

60. The Hong Kong Medical Council Professional Code and Conduct 1994.

61. *The Legal System in Hong Kong.* Department of Justice of the HKSAR 2004.

62. The website of the Equal Opportunities Commission of Hong Kong at: http://www.eoc.org.hk/eoc/GraphicsFolder/default.aspx.

63. The website of the Hong Kong Medical Council at: http://www. mchk.org.hk/.

64. The website of the Privacy Commissioner for Personal Data at: http://www.pcpd.org.hk.

65. Vincent C, Young M et al. *Why do People Sue Doctors? A Study of Patients and Relatives Taking Legal Action*. Lancet 1994; 343: 1609-1613.

66. Wilkinson Michael, Booth Christine, Cheung Eric. *The Student Guide to Civil Procedure in Hong Kong*, 2nd edn. LexisNexis 2005; Chapter 20, pp 812-854.

67. *Withholding and Withdrawing Life-prolonging Treatments: Good Practice in Decision-making* on General Medical Council's website at: http://www.gmc-uk.org/guidance/current/library/ witholding_lifeprolonging_guidance.asp.

68. Wong CY. *Who Manages Managed Care?* Singapore Medical Association News 2008; 40: 5-7.

69. *Writing References*. General Medical Council 2007 at GMC website under the List of Ethical Guidance at: http://www.gmc-uk.org/guidance/current/library/writing_references.asp.

70. Yam K. *Covert Surveillance by Law Enforcement Agencies*. Hong Kong Lawyer 2005 (09); p 33-40.

71. Yuen P. *An Analysis of the Managed Care Market in Hong Kong.* Public Policy Research Institute, the Hong Kong Polytechnic University 2007 available at: http://www.bauhinia.org/ publications/BFRC-MCO-Report.pdf.

72. 'Woman Loses Fight to Wear Cross' at website: http:// news.bbc. co.uk/1/hi/england/london/6165368.stm.

Index

The numbers in this Index refer to the chapter numbers.

283